'This ...
challengi... ...controvers... or ...
community, it should be read ... st...
committed to the glory of God in ...ship, withes ... ...rsuit
of social justice. There is ample food for thought h... ... 'by
Dr John Sentamu, Archbi... ...op of York

'This is a rare blend of sound academic exceller... ...and robust
practical experience in very insightful reflections o... ...the ministry
of black-majority churches (BMCs) in the UK. BN...Cs' leadership
must engage in rigorous ministerial training and ...eological partnership initiatives for cross-cultural effectiveness.'
Dr Daniel Akhazemea, Principal, Christ the Redeemer
College, and Chairman, RCCGUK National Advisory
Board on Education and Training

'Simultaneously challenging and encouraging, informative and
stretching, this series of lectures will do much to strengthen the
mission of black Pentecostal churches. While stimulating them to
continue to be anchored to the Rock, yet geared to twenty-first
century times here in the UK, it also offers scope for working with
others in the development of church leaders. A must-read!'
Dr Steve Brady, Principal, Moorlands College, and Chair,
Association of Bible College Principals

'The New Testament Church of God and its Oliver Lyseight Annual
Lectures have played a vital part in inspiring, encouraging and
challenging the Pentecostal tradition within the UK over the years.
The wisdom provided by the lectures and the important lessons
learned from the past will help shape the future of the Church in
this country.'
Steve Clifford, General Director, Evangelical Alliance

CHALLENGES OF BLACK PENTECOSTAL LEADERSHIP IN THE TWENTY-FIRST CENTURY

Edited by
PHYLLIS THOMPSON

First published in Great Britain in 2013

Society for Promoting Christian Knowledge
36 Causton Street
London SW1P 4ST
www.spckpublishing.co.uk

British Library Cataloguing-in-Publication Data
A catalogue record for this book is available from the British Library

ISBN 978–0–281–07028–2
eBook ISBN 978–0–281–07029–9

Typeset by Graphicraft Limited, Hong Kong
First printed in Great Britain by Ashford Colour Press
Subsequently digitally printed in Great Britain

Produced on paper from sustainable forests

*To the pioneers of the New Testament Church of God
in the UK: those who served at the forefront and
those who served behind the scenes*

Contents

Contents

Contributors

Revd Phyllis Thompson is Education Director for the New Testament Church of God. Since pioneering this role in 2007, she has been instrumental in the development and delivery of the formative ministerial and vocational enhancement for the leadership. With regard to the denomination's intent to develop confident and committed leaders, Phyllis brings a depth of experience from a wide variety of educational and training settings, both nationally and globally. She is also a published author. Her most recent piece is included in *Faith of Our Fathers* (Pathway Press, 2009).

Bishop Dr Joe Aldred is an ecumenist, published author and editor of several books. Joe works as Secretary for Minority Ethnic Christian Affairs with Churches Together in England and is a bishop in the Church of God of Prophecy. Joe is co-presenter of *Chatback*, a topical discussion programme for the African and Caribbean communities of Birmingham and the Black Country, and also presents *Pause for Thought* on BBC Radio 2 and *Prayer for the Day* on BBC Radio 4.

Dr Robert Beckford is an educator, author and award-winning broadcaster. He was the first ever tutor in black theology at Queen's College, Birmingham (1992–8) where he taught trainee priests and ministers for the Anglican and Methodist Churches. Robert is the author of five academic texts in the field of religion, culture and politics, including a study of Rastafari and Pentecostalism (*Dread and Pentecostal*, 2000), gang culture in Birmingham (*God and the Gangs*, 2004) and a theology of reggae-dub (*Jesus Dub*, 2006). His current research explores the role of documentary film as resistance to the bewitchment of black British Christianity by apoliticism and anti-intellectualism (*Documentary as Exorcism*, Continuum, 2013).

Revd Ruthlyn Bradshaw, having gained a master's degree in applied theology, is presently pursuing her doctorate at Spurgeon's College in the UK. She is the senior pastor for two branches of the New Life Assembly Fellowship of Churches, a visiting lecturer at Spurgeon's College, a lecturer at the Institute of Theology and Christian Counselling, as well as a faculty member and lecturer at the New Life Assembly Purpose-Driven School. Ruthlyn is presently completing her DMin. She is developing a pastoral response to the needs of black men struggling to reconcile their personal sexuality with their Christian contexts in black-majority churches in the UK.

Dr Elaine Storkey has lectured at Stirling University, King's College London and Oxford University. She has been a member of the General Synod of the Church of England since 1987 and President of Tearfund since 1997. She is also President of the Anglican think tank Fulcrum, and Chair of the Church and Media Network. A broadcaster and author for 25 years, she has made documentaries, written hundreds of newspaper and journal articles, and is the author of eight books, including *What's Right with Feminism* (1986), *Mary's Story, Mary's Song* (1993) and *Created or Constructed: The Great Gender Debate* (2000). Elaine received a lifetime award for services to women from the US group, Christians for Biblical Equality, in 2008. She was named as one of the top 100 female public intellectuals by *The Guardian*, and made a Templeton Journalism Fellow in 2009.

Revd Carver Anderson has been active within church life locally and regionally, and occupied the role of National Director of Youth and Christian Education for the New Testament Church of God from 1997 to 2003. He has over 30 years' experience in the fields of social, community and youth work, counselling and training, at practitioner, operational and management levels within the statutory, voluntary and community sectors. He is co-founder of Shalom Consultancy and Counselling Practice, and the Bringing Hope Charity. Carver is presently involved in completing a PhD in theology, researching issues associated with Pentecostal spirituality, including the capacity of the Holy Spirit to influence the desistance and rehabilitation of young people impacted by antisocial behaviour and gang-affiliated lifestyles.

Foreword

This book has been five years in the making. It is the result of lectures given by five eminent academics and theologians.

The lectures were delivered in memory of the founder of the New Testament Church of God (NTCG) in the United Kingdom, the late Bishop Dr Oliver A. Lyseight, who led the NTCG for the first 25 years of its existence.

Oliver Lyseight was a man of humble beginnings. He travelled from the island of Jamaica to England in the mid-1950s and set about mobilizing a disparate group of evangelical–Pentecostal believers to plant churches. Today these churches have grown to 125 congregations representing a wide cross section of UK society. There is no doubt that this is directly related to his sense of calling, leadership, vision, missionary zeal, investment in young leaders and commitment to ecumenism. If the current generation of leaders can capture some of his qualities, then the Church in general will be well on the way to fulfilling the Great Commission.

'Building Confident, Committed Leaders' is not only the first pillar of the NTCG's Big Move Programme, which is designed to equip our Church for ministry in the twenty-first century, but also the strapline of our Leadership Training Centre under whose auspices these lectures were given.

We are grateful to all our lecturers for their scholarly and masterful presentations. They each prod, provoke, stimulate and challenge us to examine our leadership inclinations and how we do ministry with reference to postmodernism and, some would argue, a post-Christian society. Their presentations, while not exhaustive, are sufficiently deep to be of interest to those dealing with contemporary issues from our Christian perspective and mission.

Pastors, Christian leaders, theologians, academics, students, researchers and those with an interest in the establishment and growth of these black-majority churches, and in particular the New Testament Church of God in the United Kingdom, should find this compendium to be a useful point of reference for the effectiveness of their ministry and work.

Eric A. Brown
Administrative Bishop
New Testament Church of God
England and Wales

Acknowledgements

Special thanks and acknowledgement to Sharon and Eustace Constance, Cliff and Monica Hill, Susan Howard, Lynn Vickery and Zenna Rose for their kind comments and helpful questions, which led to the completion of the Introduction and Conclusion of this compendium.

I also want to thank Michael Bolt for his meticulous administration throughout the five years in hosting the lectures – Michael, you are and remain a star!

Daniel Akhazemea, Stephen Brady, Steve Clifford, Neil Jameson, Lynnette Mullings and John Sentamu, your willingness to read and endorse our publication is most appreciated.

Trisha Dale, your professional advice, initial editing and encouragement have been invaluable. Thank you.

Mollie Barker, thank you for your copy-editing.

Last but not least, thanks are due to everyone who attended the lectures in 2008 through to 2012, from far and near, sometimes in the midst of adverse weather. Without your presence, questions and comments, the lectures would have been purely an academic exercise.

Introduction

PHYLLIS THOMPSON

From 2008 to 2012 the New Testament Church of God hosted a series of lectures entitled 'Challenges of black Pentecostal leadership in the UK in the twenty-first century'. They were held in memory of our founding leader in the UK, Oliver A. Lyseight, as well as to assist us at this critical stage in our growth and development. In common with many other black-majority churches here in the UK, we are now looking back on 60 formative years and wanting to build on this for the future.

At the heart of the lectures is the recognition that churches like the New Testament Church of God, established mainly in the inner cities, have shaped and framed the thinking and worldview of many of the African–Caribbean diaspora and black British people and, in more recent times, a growing number of Asian and white people. So, with pastoral sensitivity, the Oliver Lyseight lectures were hosted to provide the space for those interested in engaging in conversations about our Pentecostal heritage and the added dimension of our black British experience and how this informs our theology and mission as part of the wider Church in the UK. The lectures gave us the opportunity to examine our journey in the mode of 'pilgrims of faith seeking understanding'.

'Black Pentecostal leadership', with reference to the black Pentecostal churches, and 'black-majority churches' are terms which in their own ways denote a particular conundrum within the general Church world in the UK. What is black Pentecostalism? How does black Pentecostalism inform black theology and Christian hermeneutics, and present itself in applied theology? What do we mean by black-majority churches?

This compendium, based on the lecture series, invites the wider Church community, particularly those interested in interdenominational partnerships and the education and training of church leaders, to connect with us, to look at church leadership from our perspective, to examine together with us how the challenges we encounter in contemporary Britain interface with the legacy and the ways in which black Pentecostalism is emerging as a wing of the wider Church in contemporary Britain, and to identify key themes for leadership training and development for the benefit of our mutual witness.

All the lecturers draw from the richness of their lived experience and theological expertise to provide a candid, provocative and educative perspective on the themes they address and explore. They not only probe the issues, informing and sharpening understanding of the way the black Pentecostal churches have come to do church here in the UK, but they also challenge whether the vision is to maintain the status quo or be a prophetic Church.

The lectures have attracted an overall audience of over 500 experienced and emerging church leaders, pastors and academics, men and women, black and white Christians from across the wider Church world in England and Wales.

'The challenges of black Pentecostal leadership in the UK in the twenty-first century' by Joe Aldred

In the inaugural lecture, Joe Aldred offers a considered reflection on the theme, 'The challenges of black Pentecostal leadership in the UK in the twenty-first century', and unearths some matters pertinent to the black-majority churches, which he presents as seven key challenges. The importance of theological rigour and responsible leadership, underpinned with quality training and development, cannot be overestimated if we are to maintain and extend our credibility in the public sphere.

It may be time, he hints, for us to examine what the benefits might be for greater unity among us and those we seek to serve, in contrast to the consequences of the disparity and fragmentation of our denominational trajectories and histories. Does it seem like ecclesiological discipline, he asks, that there are so many independent Pentecostal churches operating, often in isolation from each other and the rest of the body of Christ? Conservative estimates suggest that there are well over 300 differently named churches in the UK servicing the small black constituency of approximately 2 per cent of the UK population, and approximately 6 per cent of the worshipping community.

Rather than being mere consumers of theology, Joe urges the leadership to cultivate the skills to tell their stories in their own voice and become catalysts in the educative and transformative mission and ministry in their particular context and that of the wider Church. He makes the observation that the most authoritative theologians in the world on Pentecostalism are not themselves Pentecostals. Leaders who are confident in their theological position will have a profound effect on how their congregations grow and become vibrant witnesses of the incarnate Christ in their communities. The Church without ethnic borders may well be a marker of the prophetic Church.

'From maintenance to mission: resisting the bewitchment of colonial Christianity' by Robert Beckford

Robert Beckford, in his provocative style, lays down the gauntlet for deliberation and action around the future of black Pentecostal education and makes a plea for radical commitment to serious theological education with a political nuance: a theology, he argues, that will equip the leadership and members to offer a prophetic alternative to the local and global world. He outlines his views about the Church's role as a living critique of society in solidarity with the Christian Bible. At the heart of his critique is the question of 'how the black Pentecostal church tradition in Britain might better represent God's reign on earth', and he presents a passionate argument for re-visioning the mission of the Church and discovering the transforming power of the message we proclaim. A mission he specifies is to overcome 'the institutionalization of ignorance'. An important task for contemporary leaders within the black-majority churches is one that induces people to make a deep abiding commitment to a brand of Christianity rooted in a theology that is liberating rather than oppressive, critically engaging rather than restraining, and mission-driven rather than maintenance-ridden. He discusses four stages in the quest for a prophetic alternative to passive church life. First, what he means by 'bewitchment' – the practice of witchcraft; second, what bewitchment is in relation to the act of enslavement and missionary theology's legitimation of this terror; third, the bicentennial of the abolition of the slave trade in Britain as an example of continued mass bewitchment; and finally, how theological education, or the lack of it, continues to be influenced by bewitchment tropes (themes). He asks, 'Do we black Pentecostals live with the continued impact of a missionary bewitchment?' And, 'How does this continued bewitchment impact on our value of theological education?'

'Pentecostal hermeneutics' by Ruthlyn Bradshaw

Ruthlyn Bradshaw makes a plea for credible and experienced leaders who can inspire the next generation. Pentecostals are often criticized for their unwillingness or inability to engage intentionally with the meaning of Scripture to develop their theology. The focus on the priority of Spirit baptism inadvertently belittles substantial engagement in the formation of Pentecostal hermeneutics. The challenge to us is to have clarity about how our mission to reach out to the marginalized with the gospel will inevitably cause us to give due recognition to the voices in the margins and seek to hear the biblical response to their context. With this mindset, we will raise the level of our enquiry into Scripture about what it means to uphold our belief that 'Jesus is coming soon' and at the same time clarify our understanding of how we 'do church' until he comes. Some practice of ministry is informed by inadequate hermeneutics due to the credence given to the unreliable notion,

'God said it, I believe it and that settles it.' She asserts that much work needs to be done to develop a leadership that is thoroughly trained, equipped and confident to defend the Christian faith, and she appeals to those engaged in church leadership to provide opportunities for members to examine what informs their faith and practice of ministry.

'Women in leadership' by Elaine Storkey

In the fourth lecture Elaine Storkey tackles the matter of women in leadership and applies her well-rehearsed thesis to the black-majority churches. She salutes those women who have exemplified leadership qualities and the practice of ministry against the barriers of sexism and racism. While women in leadership might be a very straightforward and uncomplicated subject, she asserts, unfortunately this is not evidenced in many of our churches. Women fill some of the highest posts in all the professions in the UK, she states, yet in the majority of our churches this is not the expectation. Women are excluded from the higher ranks of credentialled ministry, and, inadvertently, the models of leadership we present contribute to the construction of gender identity and models of leadership which are contradictory to the liberation of women into their prophetic roles in kingdom work. She sees a direct link between this reality and how we choose to read and interpret the Christian Bible and, ultimately, our view of God. She challenges us to think specifically and generally about who sets the agenda, what agenda is being set, and where we should look for endorsement for our position on women in leadership. She quite rightly asserts that 'Hermeneutics gleaned from personal emotion, psychology, culture and politics could well lead us astray'.

The key question for us, she emphasizes, is not whether the Church must catch up on the progress made for women in the rest of our culture, but what biblical theology has to say about leadership in the Church and society. Is the leadership of women endorsed by faithful Christian exegesis and is the opening up of higher offices in the Church to women compatible with the word of God? A candid reading of Scripture may lead us away from the question of whether women should be engaged in leadership to ask instead, 'What kind of woman should be encouraged into Christian leadership?'

'Youth culture: friend or foe?' by Carver Anderson

In the final lecture, Carver Anderson offers a perspective on and a framework for how our churches engage young people in the life and mission of the Church. He presents the uncomfortable truth that many young people question the validity of spirituality and the Church. They cannot hear our message in the streets where they roam, and, when they do hear us, we are more likely to proclaim a withdrawal message than one of engagement. If our leadership in this sphere of influence is to be effective it must be rooted in a theology which is practical and pastoral. A useful measure is how we show our level of care towards families, inside and outside the Church, burdened with concerns such as disaffected young people, teenage pregnancy, youth violence and antisocial behaviour, crime-, gang-, gun- and knife-associated issues, educational crises and unemployment. He further argues for a leadership that seeks to cultivate the understanding and compassion that best equip us as 'urban missionaries' engaged in a 'Pentecostal urban praxis'. Such leaders are best placed to counter the trend for our young to drift from the 'page to the streets'. Carver makes the plea for Pentecostal leaders to reclaim the radical roots of Pentecostalism to 'serve the poor, the disabled, the broken, the battered and the imprisoned'. A leadership with the ability to embrace and develop amity across the Church and social divide will be best disposed to minister to the interconnected world of our young people.

This compendium concludes with a discussion about the implications for leadership development and signposts to formative ministerial training for the wider Church leadership in the UK.

1

The challenges of black Pentecostal leadership in the UK in the twenty-first century

JOE ALDRED

Introduction

Thank you for inviting me to address you on this special occasion of the opening of the Leadership Training Centre. May I congratulate all of you on what must have been sheer hard work to get this far. I suspect there's more hard work ahead to make it a success. I pledge you my prayers and support in whatever ways I can be helpful: personally, and through my work at Churches Together in England. I have been asked to address myself to the subject, 'The challenges of black Pentecostal leadership in the UK in the twenty-first century', and I welcome the opportunity to reflect upon this important theme. I am not the first to attempt to identify and articulate the key challenges that face us, and I am sure I will not be the last. And so I come to this task humbly and prayerfully. I suspect that nothing of what I have to say will be new to some of you and certainly it will not be rocket science; however, I hope that our engagement together, with God in our midst, will bring some illumination, some new light to guide us on our way. I intend to lay before us seven key challenges, but I begin by unpacking the title of my lecture: 'The challenges of black Pentecostal leadership in the UK in the twenty-first century'.

Challenge

In contemporary parlance we can tend to view the word 'challenge' in somewhat passive terms. However, in its true meaning 'challenge' implies an invitation or summons to do something, such as take part in a contest.[1] When the Philistine champion, the giant Goliath of Gath, challenged Saul and the men of Israel with the words, 'Choose a man for yourselves, and let him come down to [fight] me' (1 Sam. 17.8), that was a challenge that demanded a response, which eventually David made, sparing King Saul's and Israel's blushes. A challenge demands a response, and if a response is not forthcoming, the contest is awarded in favour of one's opponent. So when today we speak of the challenges facing us, we are not referring to something passive, hypothetical or ephemeral; rather, we refer to matters that confront us and which demand our response. And we fail to respond at our peril.

Black Pentecostal

In the British context 'black Pentecostal' has two main meanings. First, it refers to those churches that are led and membered in the majority by people of African and Caribbean heritages.[2] Black skin colour is important in the British context because it is symbolic of a particular sociology, history and experience lived in relation to the adversity of white racism.[3] Blackness is therefore more than skin deep. Second, 'black Pentecostal' refers to the movement that is rooted in the experience iconized by Azusa Street and related revivals, which emerged around and after 1900; the five enduring identifying theological marks of such revivals, according to the *Dictionary of Pentecostal and Charismatic Movements*, are:

1 the works of grace: justification and sanctification
2 baptism in the Holy Spirit
3 premillennialism
4 healing
5 miracles.[4]

Black Pentecostalism in Britain derives from this tradition and, according to Christian Research's 2005 English Church Census, compiled by Peter Brierley, is among the fastest growing trends in an overall declining national church attendance; for example, the

New Testament Church of God showed an increase of 37 per cent in Sunday attendance between 1998 and 2005.[5] But before we get carried away, it's worth remembering that African and Caribbean people total just 2 per cent of the overall population of the UK and furthermore not all black churchgoers are Pentecostals.[6] By extrapolating from Brierley's figures, we can suggest that in 2005 51 per cent of the 300,000 Pentecostal churchgoers were black. There are at least that many black worshippers in the historic and other independent churches in the UK.

Leadership

Many are the theories on and about leadership. Here are a few popular views: some highlight the difference between a leader and a manager; some say leadership can be learned, while others say it is innate; some say God anoints you at the point of appointment, while others insist the anointing precedes the appointment. The purists speak of directive and participative leadership, task- or people-orientated leadership, transactional and transformational leadership, team leadership, and much beside. The likes of John Maxwell believe profoundly that leadership can be learned, and he provides, among other aids, a book called *The 21 Irrefutable Laws of Leadership*. It states quite simply: follow them and people will follow you.[7] Another work is his *21 Indispensable Qualities of a Leader*, with the promise that if you cultivate them you will become the person others will want to follow.[8] It may be instructive to highlight two examples from the ministry of Jesus that illustrate Christ's attitude to leadership: 'I am among you as the One who serves' (Luke 22.27); 'he calls his own sheep by name and leads them out' (John 10.3). Jesus was as much at ease leading 'among' as well as 'out in front' of his flock. Which of these models current black Pentecostal leadership mirrors is a question I leave for further discussion!

The twenty-first century

I want to use four terms to describe the twenty-first century: post-modern, postcolonial, post-denominational and post-Christendom.

Postmodern

John Drane observes that Western civilization, based upon European Enlightenment values, has three philosophical facets: rationalism, which asserts that the only things worth knowing are what we can think about in particular analytical and abstract ways; materialism, which asserts that the only things worth thinking about are those we can see, touch and handle; and reductionism, which asserts that everything can be understood by taking it to pieces.[9] These three concepts of rationalism, materialism and reductionism constitute the basic philosophical foundation of postmodernity. The word describes also the abolition or erosion of conventional certainties, replacing them with a new pluralism in an exciting world of endless possibilities and uncertainties. Walter Brueggemann argues that a postmodern climate recognizes that there is no given definition (of anything) and that rival claims must simply be argued out. Conversely, modernity was a time when everybody knew their place and stayed there; the slave, the servant and the poor knew their place beneath the slave master, the lord of the manor and the rich, and stayed there. Brueggemann calls this a period of 'certitude and domination', and cites Karl Marx, who astutely observed that the ruling ideas of each age have ever been the ideas of its ruling class.[10] Since I and my sort were never part of that ruling class, I do not clamour for the return of modernity; I merely observe that everything is up for grabs.

Postcolonial

A second signifier of the twenty-first century is the term 'post-colonial'. This identifies a period after imperialistic colonial rule, particularly in relation to the UK and her former colonies in Africa, Asia and the Caribbean. However, as Anthony Reddie and Michael Jagessar point out, 'postcolonial' is not about the demise of colonialism as 'post', or past, since it embodies both 'after' and 'beyond'; it's not just about historical chronologies, but more about adopting a critical stance, oppositional tactic or subversive strategy.[11] Within postcolonialism is, according to R. S. Sugirtharajah, an ongoing battle for emancipation, and a continuing battle to dismantle imperial institutions and dominating structures.[12] And so this postcolonial space is a problematic one, because as Musa W. Dube points out, our current relationships involve the colonizer and the colonized, the ruler and the ruled, the centre and the periphery, the Global North and the Global South.[13] There may even be resonance here too with the relationship between some churches' general headquarters and their outposts.

Post-denominational

A third signifier of the twenty-first century is the term 'post-denominational'. As with the other two themes, 'post-denominational' does not describe the absence of denominations; rather it describes a time when the power and rule of sectarian denominationalism is under serious question and strain as Christian belonging depends upon new and alternative factors. I remember when I sang, with gusto, a local denominational ditty:

> Church of Prophecy,
> Church of Prophecy is my belief,
> Church of Prophecy till I die;
> I was born and bred Church of Prophecy
> And I'll die on the Prophecy side.

I would not sing that now. 'Post-denominational' describes a period when the old certainties of sectarian boundaries are waning and some have all but vanished. The names are still there and new ones emerge every day, but the people so gathered under these various banners are increasingly seeing themselves as part of the *ekklesia*, less as the property of a denomination or person.[14] It may be that one way to understand our post-denominational times is by applying Rick Warren's 'spiritual surfing' theory. Here, people look for where the wave of God is and surf there, rather than join those trying to build waves.[15] It may also be the case that denominational ties have been replaced by the cult of personalities and that Christians now divide their loyalties between denominations, personalities, ministries and ecumenical streams. What is not in doubt is that things ain't what they used to be. As Hans Küng puts it, the future has already begun; he further argues that, even if the Church wanted to, it cannot stand aside from this worldwide reorientation which heralds a new era. Küng does, however, offer this hope: 'what looks like a serious crisis may mark the moment of new life; what looks like a sinister threat may in reality be a great opportunity'.[16]

Post-Christendom

If this is a moment of opportunity, then it occurs against a background of not just postmodernity, postcolonialism and post-denominationalism, but also post-Christendom. Although it is true that Christianity is growing in the Global South, it is also true that in the Western world, where we live, Christianity as the contemporary cornerstone of custom, morals and culture is a thing of the past or at best on the wane. In its place are myriad faiths and spiritualities and a rampant, strident atheism: the 'death of God' brigade.

John Drane asserts simply but profoundly that we are in the midst of a paradigm shift of massive proportions. Drane reminds us that when nineteenth-century philosopher Friedrich Nietzsche spoke of the death of God he implied the disintegration of the entire religio-philosophical basis upon which Western civilization had been built. He describes this regressive process in the following way: that in the earliest times humans sacrificed each other to the gods, then later they sacrificed their instincts and nature to the gods, and in a third and final stage they sacrificed God, leaving nothing to worship save stone, stupidity, gravity and fate.[17] I hope I am not painting too gloomy a picture of our times; I am merely attempting to present a picture of the context in which this Leadership Training Centre is being raised up by God in the New Testament Church of God, in black Pentecostalism, in the Church in the UK.

A nation that has rejected God

Sometimes I feel as though I live in the nation upon which woe was pronounced because they forgot God and called evil good and good evil, darkness light and light darkness, bitter sweet and sweet bitter (Isa. 5.20). Sometimes it feels like the time referred to in Romans 1.18–21: 'For the wrath of God is revealed from heaven against all ungodliness and unrighteousness of men, who suppress the truth in unrighteousness . . . because, although they knew God, they did not glorify Him as God.' I scarcely need remind you of the spiritual, social, political and economic chaos we are in locally, nationally and internationally. There are numerous international political and economic wars and intra-national tribal conflicts; 10 per cent of the world consumes 90 per cent of the world's resources, with millions dying in abject poverty; the phenomenon of globalization means that multinational companies backed by unfair trade arrangements keep the rich rich and the poor poor.

A report by Iain Duncan Smith, titled *Breakdown Britain*, highlights issues such as family breakdowns, educational failure, worklessness and economic dependence, addictions and indebtedness among our ills; then there is the little fact that our kids are lost, being killed and killing each other on our streets.[18] Is it any wonder that some now view the Church and particularly the black Church as the last hope of redemption for this country? As someone told me recently, 'It's only the Church that can help us now!' And some of our own have articulated what a few of these challenges are; let me name three.

First, Robert Beckford continues to argue that the black Church must develop a political theology and praxis, and not allow notions of transcendence through rapturous music, singing and preaching to foster political ignorance and naivety.[19] Second, Anthony Reddie has argued for the black Church to develop an education programme that is liberative, providing people with the tools to survive in a racialized environment.[20] We do not need a form of

education that simply creates clones, and obedient denominational cadres. Third, Mark Sturge has laid down the challenges
of credibility and integrity, relevance, confidence, spiritual impact,
inspiring young people and punching above our weight in the
public square.[21] Many others from inside and outside have
challenged the black Pentecostal Church, yet it remains to be seen
whether we have the stomach for the fight. Have we the will to
move from maintenance to mission? On the assumption that my
part-rhetorical question attracts a 'Yes', I want to name seven
clear challenges that I believe demand answers. I posit them in
the hope that this Leadership Training Centre will help facilitate
an articulate and spiritual response to them.

The historical challenge

The historical challenge that is before us begins with the repeated
biblical imperative to 'remember'. For example, Exodus 13.3: 'And
Moses said to the people: "Remember this day in which you went
out of Egypt, out of the house of bondage; for by strength of hand
the LORD brought you out of this place."' Here, as elsewhere, the root
meaning of 'remember' is to 'mention'. So the historic challenge
to remember requires that we find ways to mention important
people, happenings and things. This calls for a change of vocabulary and iconography, because what we say, iconize and celebrate
illustrates everything about the value we place or do not place on
what has gone before, and its influence on our future direction. The
Jamaican hero Marcus Garvey has said that history is the landmark
by which we are directed into the true course of life.[22] However,
it is not only important that history is told; it also matters who
tells it. Richard Reddie reminds us of an African proverb: 'Until
lions have their own historians, the story of the hunt will always
glorify the hunter.'[23] History is somebody's story, and that somebody is almost always the victor; rarely does the victim's story
get told. Black Pentecostal leaders of a people whose history goes
largely untold, or badly told, have a responsibility to develop a

vocabulary and an iconography that mentions and marks their history appropriately. Equally, our focus on history must include a new vocabulary about the historical Jesus, a first-century Galilean Jew, not an eighteenth-century European.

Our responsibility to rootless African Caribbean youth

I am in little doubt that a key problem affecting our young people today is a lack of identity linked to a lack of familiarity with their history: where they come from, the morals, spirituality and values upon which their communities were built, the heroes and 'sheroes' upon whose shoulders they stand, and the struggles and victories they fought and either learned from or won. The identity needs of our young place upon us a historical challenge. Indeed, I beg to suggest that, as Robin Walker has recently articulated, the history of the human race needs to be retold, properly.[24] The bicentenary of the parliamentary act to abolish the slave trade is a timely reminder of how history needs to, and can, be revised. At the start of 2007, when asked who they most associated with ending the enslavement of Africans, overwhelmingly people, black and white, named William Wilberforce. However, marking the bicentenary has made manifest a better-balanced historical recounting of this epoch of human tragedy.

We now know that the story of the enslavement and liberation is not primarily one of white European poacher turned gamekeeper, but that resistance in many forms was waged by the enslaved themselves during and after capture.[25] We now know that black people and white people worked tirelessly for an end to that shameful episode in human history, that millions of Africans lost or gave their lives, and that many lived to tell their own stories, chief among them Olaudah Equiano.[26] Through the cooperative leadership of government, ecumenical bodies, human rights organizations and individuals, no longer have black children in schools to hang their heads in shame when they see pictures of their enslaved ancestors. Rather they can hold their heads high in the knowledge that the reason they are here is because their fore parents were made of such sturdy stuff, physically and in character, that they survived that onslaught of man's inhumanity to man.

The Church and the Pentecostal movement

We in the black Pentecostal movement forget at our peril the importance of our complex history; a history that, unless explained, leaves successive generations rootless and in a crisis of identity. The history of the Church needs to be told, properly, including the little spat back in the 1920s between what we now know as (New Testament) Church of God and Church of God of Prophecy. We cannot any longer afford histories such as those told in *Upon This Rock* and *Like a Mighty Army*, which serve to divide us; for only when I had read them both did I get a balanced view of the major dispute that split our forerunners and still splits us today.[27]

The historical challenge requires us also to recount the way in which race has played a significant part in our development, dividing Christians along Jim Crow lines, and we need to come clean on how it is that the strong have not always fought for the dignity of our fellow humans and fellow believers in Christ.[28] Of course, our true roots are in Christ, but a lot of subversive transplanting and replanting has taken place, and we need to revise and retell our history, for liberation and clarity, demonstrating whose historic shoulders we really do stand on. Some tough historical questions need asking and answering, such as: How and why was William Seymour abandoned by the movement he established? Why was it that as late as 1958 Oliver Lyseight's appointment as National Overseer required a change in the governance regulations of the Church of God, Cleveland?[29] We have a historical challenge to respond to.

The theological challenge

A second challenge before us is a theological one. Some years ago I mentioned to a fellow young brother that I was contemplating studying theology. To this he replied that he did not think we should do theology; we should just stick to the Bible. Black Pente-costals need to lose their theology-phobia. Theology, it has been variously pointed out, is what we all do when we reflect upon God and the world God has created. We must never trivialize the need to engage in this reflection properly. If we are going to think about God, we had better think deeply and well. If we are going to share our thoughts with others, we had better check and double-check that what we are saying is as correct as we know how to make it. Never forget, it is truth that sets people free, not well-rehearsed dogma. As Paul told Timothy, 'Be diligent to present yourself approved to God, a worker who does not need to be ashamed, rightly dividing the word of truth' (2 Tim. 2.15). James Cone states that

> Theology is the critical side of faith, and without it faith loses its dis-tinctive identity . . . if a church has no theologians, then it cannot be genuinely self-critical and thereby seek to overcome its short-comings and weaknesses. Black churches have not encouraged the development of theology alongside strong emphasis on preaching.[30]

Cone speaks here in rather exclusive terms, and his focus is the black Church in the United States. However, there is a strong resonance with the black Pentecostal Church in the UK. It certainly chimes with my experience. But we should trust our own people more, not less, to critique ourselves. This way we build confidence and trust.

The theological challenge we face is both external and internal. Our greatest fear seems linked to academic theological studies. I understand the fear, especially after I heard the joke about the young priest who took his Bible with him as he went to Oxford to study theology and graduated wondering what to do with it! But we need to bridge the gap between us in the Church and our colleagues in the academy, especially those in the field of black theology. There is in the UK a thriving black-theology commun-ity that operates at arm's length from black Pentecostal leadership. I know because I have been there at some important points in our journey, including my spell as the founding chair of the *Journal of Black Theology* in Britain, launched in 1998. We have tried in vain to attract black Pentecostals to subscribe to the journal or write in it. The journal has now gone international, is published three times a year and is recognized as the main vehicle of black-theological thought in the world, and it comes out of the UK. I am desperate for the black Pentecostal community to take owner-ship of it. It probably does not help the cause when the current editor of the journal suggests that the theological work done by 'Black evangelicals' falls into the realm of 'Black Christian reli-gious experience', not black theology.[31] According to Reddie, 'Black Christian religious experience' is a 'folk orientated approach' which, while it arises from the black experience, does not necessarily have a political or explicitly transformative agenda, or see blackness as a primary hermeneutical lens for reinterpreting the Christian faith. This, he argues, puts us at odds with black theology, which begins with the material reality of the black experience as its point of departure.

There clearly is an ideological chasm that requires a bridge. Sitting in both camps, as I try to do, I suggest that a possible way forward is the recognition that the Bible and black experience are not in opposition; rather they exist in dialectical tension in relation to the person of Christ. Most probably, it is because Pentecostals have been resistant to structural engagement with academic theology that the most authoritative theologians in the world on Pentecostalism, such as Professor Walter Hollenweger, are not themselves Pente-costals.[32] It is not that there are no Pentecostals doing theology, or that there is something innately wrong with non-Pentecostals doing Pentecostal theology, but there is here a challenge for us.

It is probably a little unfair but not far from the truth to say that Pentecostals, especially black Pentecostals, love doctrine; they do not love theology. Doctrines tend to be prescriptive and agreed upon by people long enough ago for us not to have to think things through in our day. We just enforce them, often like the Pharisees and sometimes just as harshly. Unfortunately, a protectionist environ-ment towards doctrines tends to discourage theological investiga-tion and examination. This often leads to the creation of blind leaders of the blind, where the outcome is not enlightenment and wholeness but rather a falling headlong into the ditch of ignorance and frustration. For example, as evangelical Christians, we instinctively object to homosexuality, but where do we make the theological case for our objection based on Scripture, reason, history, Christian tradition and divine revelation? Where do we reflect upon the different doctrinal emphases of Charles Fox Parham and William Seymour about initial evidence?[33] Where do we reflect upon prosperity teachings and tithing? What do we make of a two-stage or three-stage salvific process? Is it really the case that all we are allowed to do is passively accept and propagate only that which is handed down from on high, or can we innovate theological reasoning as befitting a people with lively minds and who follow a limitless God that is past finding out? There is need for a space that does more than assent to givens. Guarding the faith implies more than unquestioning guardianship; it implies a rigorous attention to biblical theological truth and a willingness to look again, and again, to see if the things we have been taught are true (Acts 17.11).

In the UK, black theologian Robert Beckford has attempted some reconstruction of black Pentecostal theology, focusing on how it can be politicized. Beckford makes the point that black Pentecostalism is not a unitary system or homogeneous practice; rather, it is a dynamic tradition consisting of a legion of denominations and congregations bearing the theological hallmarks of the experience of God, a dynamic spirituality and empowering worship.[34] This empowering worship, however, is not matched, in Beckford's view, by effectiveness in the political and economic spheres. Emmanuel Lartey's seven-item agenda for black theology in the UK is also something for us to consider. Lartey posits the following:

1 a biblical hermeneutical task that builds upon black love of the 'Word';
2 a historical task that articulates the trajectories of black people in the UK;

3 a philosophical and cultural educational task that unearths and articulates African and Asian philosophies;
4 a socio-economic task that emphasizes the holistic nature of humanity;
5 a political task that is committed to the struggle for justice;
6 a psychological task that connects with black understanding, thereby raising self-esteem, leading to good mental health;
7 an aesthetic task that promotes black arts in music, drama, dance, film and iconography.[35]

I believe formal theological and ministerial training to be of the utmost importance, not just for the benefit of gaining a piece of paper, but also for a much higher purpose. Writing at the beginning of the twentieth century, the African American W. E. B. DuBois, reflecting upon the role of education in the rehabilitation of the 'Negro Race' (*sic*) after the trauma of enslavement, reminds us about the real purpose of education and training. He describes the need for 'an education that encourages aspiration, that sets the loftiest of ideals and seeks as an end culture and character'.[36] My call is for home-grown theologians to be encouraged to emerge from within the black Pentecostal movement, people who are liberated to reflect and write critically, people of such character that they assist in the process of developing an authentic black British Pentecostal theology that helps us to remain as relevant in the twenty-first century as we were in the twentieth. Here I note the words of Bishop Eric Brown in the Leadership Training Centre prospectus: 'to lead effectively in the twenty-first century, leaders must be trained and well disciplined'.[37]

The ecclesiological challenge

Another challenge that faces us is the ecclesiological one. Ecclesiology concerns the shape of church, and according to Alister McGrath it asks questions like: 'what sort of body is the church?'[38] The Bible offers us many images of the Church as a bride, the building of God, the people of God, a holy temple, the body of Christ, and as a multi-membered body (1 Cor. 12.12). The early development of this complex entity was racked with controversies and persecution, accompanied by rapid growth and expansion. In spite of everything, one accompanying feature of the Church over those years, however, was a sense of order, organization and authority. And while we must acknowledge that black Pentecostalism emerged out of a Nonconformist tradition, birthed by people who were expressing both their dissatisfaction with the status quo and, simultaneously, following where God was leading, I do believe we have to ask ourselves if the present shape or shapelessness of black Pentecostalism in the UK fits the biblical model, marked by diversity within a framework of order.

Hans Küng makes the sobering point, albeit from a Roman Catholic perspective, that the nature and form given to the Church, through God's eschatological saving act in Christ, was given it as a responsibility. This nature, he says, must be constantly realized anew and given new form in history by our personal action of faith.[39] A challenge to us is this: How well does what we currently are match the ecclesiological remit of one, holy, catholic and apostolic Church?[40] Permit me to ask another question: Does it seem like ecclesiological discipline that there are so many independent Pentecostal churches operating, often in isolation from each other and the rest of the body of Christ? Conservative estimates suggest there are well over 300 differently named churches in the UK servicing the small black constituency of approximately 2 per cent of the UK population, and approximately 6 per cent of the worshipping community.[41] Does this pass for diversity, or fragmentation?

The challenge for us is clear: it is the task of constructing a spiritual and rational argument for closer working together, and mergers of organizations may be necessary. Pentecostal leadership cannot afford simply to stand back and look on at the fragmentation. Someone must be willing to articulate a prophetic vision of our life together, now and in the future, that inspires action towards greater unity. Since we are one Church, we had better start behaving like it. In a time past in Israel, the sons of Issachar were said to have understanding of their times, 'to know what Israel ought to do' (1 Chron. 12.32). Do we?

The ecumenical challenge

The ecumenical challenge is a major one, and includes, for example, black–black ecumenism, black–white and multicultural ecumenism, internationalist ecumenism, and working with ecumenical agencies; some would even argue for consideration to be given to inter-faith relations between the three major Abrahamic faiths. We need to act because the unity prayed for by Jesus in John 17 continues to challenge and embarrass us profoundly, and yet I often wonder how much we understand it. In a transcendent sense, that which God utters exists; what we are challenged by is how we express and actualize that which already is, but it is difficult to rise above our understanding of what we are trying to do. If, as is often the case, we believe that unity means a single denomination with a single human head, be that the Pope or another type of leader, then we will continue to strive for what some call the visible unity of the one universal catholic Church. If on the other hand we perceive unity as something first and foremost of the spirit, then we will focus less on visible disunity as something to fix and instead work towards keeping the unity of the spirit in the bond of peace (see Eph. 4.3), in a manner that leaves differences intact. As Joel Edwards points out, the whole universe is one gigantic symphony of 'harmonising differences', from the vast expanse of our galaxies to the individuality of each delicate snowflake.[42] Unity in diversity is, I believe, implied in Jesus' prayer: '[make them] one as We are' (John 17.11).

The place we pursue is a place of spiritual maturity and spiritual bondedness, of redeemed diversity, that is devoid of the three traits of divisiveness that Mark Sturge highlights: the lack of unity and joined-up mission, the undermining of trust, and the evasion of mutual acceptance.[43] The Scriptures put it like this: 'till we all come to the unity of the faith and the knowledge of the Son of God, to a perfect man' (Eph. 4.13). Being one as the Godhead is one is well beyond what a single denomination in the world could achieve. We all know only too well how much fussing and fighting goes on within our single denominations to believe that doing that on a grander scale would solve anything! Whatever our theological stance on secondary, even sometimes primary, issues, the place we seek is one where in spirit we are so much one that the world sees you in me and me in you; that the world marvels and says, 'Look how they love one another!'[44] It is by this that the world will know that we are who we say we are, and be led to glorify God. This unity is counter-cultural and counter-intuitive because it crosses and redeems race, culture, clan, nationality and sectarianism. It's a unity predicated upon the person of Christ as God, Lord of all, the focus of our worship and work. This Leadership Training Centre's task is to assist in raising up 'a living household (*oikos*) in which all God's children who have been beaten down or excluded by the powers of this world find their rightful place'.[45] But some ecumenists tell us that the magnitude of our task is illustrated by the fact that 'the churches involved in the ecumenical movement have not only been divided; they have been divided over what it would mean to be united'.[46]

The social, economic and political challenge

Some years ago a former national overseer of the New Testament Church of God, Selwyn Arnold, published the result of his doctoral thesis that examined the Church's response to social responsibility.[47] Arnold challenged the black Pentecostal Church to hold on to its vigorous belief in the concept of the afterlife while simultaneously developing policies, strategies and plans to attend to the everyday issues of people's lives in the here and now. His thesis was titled, 'Why Wait for Tomorrow?' Echoing Joel Edwards' call from an earlier time, that we need to both preach to the people on Sunday and accompany them to the police station on Monday when their children get into trouble, Arnold highlights the image of a minister who could walk into the shops where the drug pushers were hanging out and be recognized as someone from the church who was making a difference in the community.[48]

Then in 2003 Christian Aid, in collaboration with the University of Birmingham, published a report titled *Am I My Brother and Sister's Keeper?* to highlight the lack of and the possibility of black Church economic development.[49] Jesus' example of healing the sick, feeding the hungry, including the excluded and tackling oppressive powers head on seems an excellent pointer to the Church's social, economic and political ministry in the world. I note that in the early phase of the black Church in the UK the charge that we were insular, looking only after our members and then only concerned with social welfare, not political activity, had some veracity. However, as Berrisford Lewis in a recent unpublished thesis has sought to show, black church leaders are heavily involved in political engagement.[50] This growing level of engagement in strategic high-level politics is emerging in numerous ways, significantly through the work of the Black Christian Leaders' Forum. This new forum meets regularly with cabinet ministers and civil servants to advocate for issues of importance to the black community.

As we look ahead, a key to the black Pentecostal Church's socio-economic and political involvement in the world will be the mobilization of our members. However, to enable this, members must feel liberated to act. Galatians 5.1 illustrates how Christians easily become unsettled, and are therefore in constant need of guidance and support to stay in the freedom of Christ, freedom from the bondage of legalism. Unity and effective engagement in the world can only be achieved when our people realize their freedom in Christ, becoming free from rules imposed by other people, free from fear of self and others, liberated to be who and what God intended each and every person to be. Paul puts it simply: 'It is for freedom that Christ has set us free' (Gal. 5.1 NIV). Here I believe we have a lot to learn from black and liberation theology. James Cone reminds us that freedom is the structure of, and a movement in, historical existence.[51] Freedom has to be real and holistic, true to the past and the future. It's no good freeing people from slavery, then enslaving them in colonialism; no good freeing them spiritually by giving them the Bible, while enslaving them by using the same Bible to coerce them into servitude. The indomitable human spirit that instinctively desires freedom will always protest oppression and enslavement. That is why the enslaved sang,

> Oh Freedom! Oh Freedom!
> Oh Freedom, I love thee!
> And before I'll be a slave, I'll be buried in my grave
> And go home to my Lord and be free.[52]

If I may cite Cone again, he says that 'freedom expresses God's will to be in relation to his creatures in the social context of their striving for the fulfillment of humanity'.[53] Neither can we afford the luxury of narrowness in our reference to humanity – we cannot mean black humanity, since until all are free, none is free. We are called to a universal concept of mission to the world, not just to people who look like us.

The leadership challenge

As I mentioned before, there is no single definition, type or style of leadership. However, for me the stand-out feature of leadership is the ability to lead people into a fruitful future. People are always asking, 'Where are we going?' 'Where are you taking us?' And so a key challenge for black Pentecostal leadership is the vision thing. The wisdom literature says simply, 'Where there is no vision, the people perish' or 'Where there is no revelation, the people cast off restraint' (Prov. 29.18 KJV and NKJV respectively). That is, if we do not help people understand their context, their present and their future, they will behave with carelessness and abandonment. It is the discipline of the task or the journey that keeps us focused and productive.

Another aspect of leadership that challenges us was highlighted in a limited inquiry I commissioned in 2005. This showed that although our membership is overwhelmingly female, our pastoral ministry is overwhelmingly male: 83 per cent. Probably even more alarming was the revelation that only 3 per cent of those involved in pastoral ministry were under 40 years old, a whopping 80 per cent were between 40 and 65 years old, and 17 per cent were over 65. These statistics, if true, signal real questions about succession planning. Our traditional system, in which leaders emerge and are then home-trained, leaves too much variability in the system. This needs to be supplemented by a commitment to high-level training and development programmes, with our top leaders mentoring others who are emerging as well as those in office. It is no coincidence that the great leaders of our time have been and are educated people: Martin Luther King, with an earned doctorate; Nelson Mandela, a lawyer; Barack Obama, a lawyer;[54] Condoleeza Rice, with an earned PhD; Diane Abbott MP, Baroness Amos, Baroness Scotland, David Lammy, Joel Edwards, and more, are university graduates. It's OK to get your education at the cross, but you must then go on to study and train. So, as our pioneers go off the stage one by one, where are their replacements?

The missiological challenge

The seventh challenge that I suggest lies before us is one concerning mission. I have never forgotten the many leaders I interviewed during my PhD research, who declared unequivocally that they believed God had brought black Christians to the UK to bring about revival in a country in which the Christian Church was in, or heading towards, an apostate state.[55] Sadly, 60 years on, it does not appear that mainstream Christianity has been rescued, but our mission to hold the Bible high, resist racism and refuse to compromise the gospel as we understood it was and is very clear. Clear too was our sense of mission to seek out and rescue the lost from among us. Oliver Lyseight, for example, makes clear in his autobiography that he was personally quite comfortable in a material sense, but it was observing his fellow Caribbean people with nowhere to worship that motivated him to start the mission in Wolverhampton.[56] However, having passed that formative stage of mission, our membership now grows from immigration and migration, not from converts from the mainstream population.

The question is: What shape must the ministry of the black Pentecostal Church take to be effective and relevant in the twenty-first century? Mark Sturge devotes a section of his book, *Look What the Lord Has Done!*, to discussing the future of black-majority churches. He concludes that he does not know what the future holds for this genre of church; nobody knows or can know.[57] I suggest that, while the future is in God's mind, it may be permissible to say that the future of black Pentecostal churches depends on their missiological positioning. Having initiated churches that did not exist in the UK before, and by so doing, rescued people who did not find a home or did not desire one in the historic churches, the second phase of our existence has been to become more sociologically, economically and politically secured and relevant. However, I suggest that a third phase of our churches' development ought to be mainstreaming ourselves so that we minister to, and draw a following from, non-black, non-African and non-Caribbean heritage communities. A mission predicated on a gospel and ministry to the world rather than one that is ethnic-specific is more likely to underwrite our future existence in an increasingly sceptical and unbelieving Western world. We cannot continue to fish among 2 per cent of all the fish in the sea!

Conclusion

I have tried to set out some of the challenges that face the leadership of the black Pentecostal churches in the UK. In the face of all of these, this Leadership Training Centre cannot afford to think and build small. It cannot think only of the New Testament Church of God, or of the black Pentecostal churches alone, but must also think of providing a ministry to the Church as a whole. For black Pentecostal leadership in the twenty-first century, the task amounts to this:

> prepar[ing] God's people for works of service, so that the body of Christ may be built up until we all reach unity in the faith and in the knowledge of the Son of God and become mature, attaining to the whole measure of the fulness of Christ.
>
> (Eph. 4.12–13 NIV1984)

It is a tall order; are we up to it?

Notes

1 See *Collins English Dictionary*, 6th edn, Glasgow: HarperCollins, 2003.
2 Some Asians may consider themselves part of this definition too.
3 Emmanuel Lartey (ed.), *Black Theology in Britain: A Journal of Contextual Praxis*, no. 1, Sheffield: Sheffield Academic Press (1998), pp. 7–9.
4 Stanley Burgess and Gary McGee (eds), *Dictionary of Pentecostal and Charismatic Movements*, Grand Rapids, MI: Zondervan, 1993, p. 2.
5 Peter Brierley, *Pulling out of the Nose Dive*, London: Christian Research, 2006, p. 33.
6 1991 UK Census <www.statistics.gov.uk/cci/nugget.asp?id=273>. A further 1.2 per cent are of mixed heritage, some of whom are African or Caribbean and another ethnicity.
7 John C. Maxwell, *The 21 Irrefutable Laws of Leadership*, Nashville: Thomas Nelson, 1998.
8 John C. Maxwell, *The 21 Indispensable Qualities of a Leader*, Nashville: Thomas Nelson, 1999.
9 John Drane, *Cultural Change and Biblical Faith*, Carlisle: Paternoster Press, 2000, p. 129.
10 Walter Brueggemann, *The Bible and Postmodern Imagination*, London: SCM Press, London, 1993, pp. vii–3.
11 Michael Jagessar and Anthony Reddie (eds), *Postcolonial Black British Theology: New Textures and Themes*, Peterborough: Epworth Press, 2007, p. xvii.
12 R. S. Sugirtharajah, *Postcolonial Criticism and Biblical Interpretation*, Oxford: Oxford University Press, 2002, p. 25.

13 Musa W. Dube, 'Reading for Decolonisation (John 4.1–42)', in Musa
    W. Dube and Jeffrey L. Stanley (eds), *John and Postcolonialism: Travel,
    Space and Power*, London: Sheffield Academic Press, 2002, pp. 51–75.

14 W. Ward Gasque, 'The Church in the New Testament', in David J.
    Ellis and W. Ward Gasque, *In God's Community*, Wheaton, IL: Harold
    Shaw, 1979, pp. 1–13.

15 Rick Warren, *Purpose Driven Church: Growth without Compromising
    Your Message and Mission*, Grand Rapids, MI: Zondervan, 1995, p. 13.

16 Hans Küng, *The Church*, Tunbridge Wells: Burns & Oates, 1995, p. 3.

17 Drane, *Cultural Change*, p. 175.

18 Social Justice Policy Group (Chair: Rt Hon. Iain Duncan Smith MP),
    Breakdown Britain: Interim Report on the State of the Nation, London:
    December 2006 <www.centreforsocialjustice.org.uk/client/downloads/
    CSJ%20FINAL%20(2).pdf>.

19 Robert Beckford, *Dread and Pentecostal: A Political Theology for the
    Black Church in Britain*, London: SPCK, 2000, p. 182.

20 Anthony G. Reddie, *Nobodies to Somebodies: A Practical Theology for
    Education and Liberation*, Peterborough: Epworth Press, 2003.

21 Mark Sturge, *Look What the Lord Has Done!*, Bletchley: Scripture
    Union, 2005, pp. 211–24.

22 Amy Jacques-Garvey (ed.), *Philosophy and Opinions of Marcus Garvey*,
    New York: Atheneum, 1992, p. 1.

23 Richard S. Reddie, *Abolition! The Struggle to Abolish Slavery in the
    British Colonies*, Oxford: Lion Hudson, 2007, p. 33.

24 Robin Walker, *When We Ruled*, London: Every Generation Media, 2006.

25 Reddie, *Nobodies*, p. 110.

26 Olaudah Equiano, *The Interesting Narrative and Other Writings*
    (ed. Vincent Carretta), London: Penguin, 2003.

27 C. T. Davidson, *Upon This Rock*, vol. 1, Cleveland, TN: White Wing,
    1973; C. W. Conn, *Like a Mighty Army: A History of the Church of
    God 1886–1976*, Cleveland, TN: Pathway Press, 1977.

28 David Michel, *Telling the Story: Black Pentecostals in the Church of
    God*, Cleveland, TN: Pathway Press, 2000.

29 J. D. Aldred, *Respect: Understanding Caribbean British Christianity*,
    Peterborough: Epworth Press, 2005, p. 96.

30 James Cone, *My Soul Looks Back*, New York: Orbis Books, 1993,
    pp. 70, 71.

31 Michael N. Jagessar and Anthony G. Reddie, *Black Theology in Britain: A Reader*, London: Equinox, 2007, p. 3.

32 Walter J. Hollenweger, *Pentecostalism: Origins and Developments Worldwide*, Peabody, MA: Hendrickson, 1997.

33 Hollenweger, *Pentecostalism*, p. 20.

34 Beckford, *Dread and Pentecostal*.

35 Emmanuel Lartey (ed.), *Black Theology in Britain: A Journal of Contextual Praxis*, no. 3, Sheffield: Sheffield Academic Press (1999), pp. 79–91.

36 W. E. B. DuBois, *The Souls of Black Folk*, New York: Dover, 1994, pp. 58, 59.

37 New Testament Church of God, Leadership Training Centre Prospectus, 2008.

38 Alister McGrath, *Christian Theology: An Introduction*, Oxford: Blackwell, 1994, p. 405.

39 Hans Küng, *The Church*, Tunbridge Wells: Burns & Oates, 1968, p. 263.

40 McGrath, *Christian Theology*, pp. 418–26.

41 See <www.bmcdirectory.co.uk>.

42 Joel Edwards, *Lord, Make Us One but Not All the Same*, London: Hodder & Stoughton, 1999, p. 114.

43 Sturge, *Look*, p. 168.

44 Tertullian, *The Apology* 39.7.

45 Michael Kinnamon and Brian E. Hope (eds), *The Ecumenical Movement: An Anthology of Key Texts and Voices*, Grand Rapids, MI: Eerdmans, 1997, p. 1.

46 Kinnamon and Hope (eds), *Ecumenical Movement*, p. 79.

47 S. E. Arnold, *From Scepticism to Hope*, Nottingham: Grove Books, 1992.

48 Arnold, *From Scepticism*, p. 73.

49 Maxine Howell-Baker and Tonya Brown (eds), *Am I My Brother and Sister's Keeper?*, London: Christian Aid, 2003.

50 Berrisford Lewis, 'African-Caribbean Pentecostal Church Leaders and Socio-Political Engagement in Contemporary Britain', University of Birmingham, 2008.

51 James Cone, *God of the Oppressed*, San Francisco, CA: HarperSanFrancisco, 1975, p. 11.

52 Post-Civil War African American freedom song, author unknown, quoted in Cone, *Oppressed*, p. 11.

53 Cone, *Oppressed*, p. 139.

54 Read their autobiographies: Nelson Mandela, *The Long Walk to Freedom*, London: Little, Brown and Co., 1994; Barack Obama, *The Audacity of Hope*, New York: Canongate, 2007.

55 See J. D. Aldred, *Respect: Understanding Caribbean British Christianity*, Peterborough: Epworth Press, 2005.

56 Oliver Lyseight, *Forward March: An Autobiography*, Willenhall: Birches Printers, 1995.

57 Sturge, *Look*, p. 206.

2

From maintenance to mission: resisting the bewitchment of colonial Christianity

ROBERT BECKFORD

Introduction

I want to begin by thanking you for inviting me to contribute to this prestigious lecture series. I hope that my paper will be as stimulating as last year's presentation by Bishop Joe Aldred. His paper makes it possible to situate this offering as a continuation of the debate around the future of black Pentecostal education. As African American theologian James Cone once said, during a visit to the UK in the mid-1990s, the task of the theologian is to be 'critical of the church'.[1] My interpretation of Cone on the task of the theologian is that theologians are to be in critical solidarity with the Church. So I offer this paper as someone who loves God, is part of the liberating work of the kingdom, but thinks that the black Church could and should be doing a lot better.

My academic work is in the field of religion and culture. To put it simply, I am interested in the multiplicity of ways that Christianity and culture converge and diverge in religious history. I look at these interactions through a variety of lenses, including those of my slave and colonial fore parents who possessed perspectives that I believe we can learn from in the present.[2] Today, in this paper, I will continue to combine theology and culture in this vein by working with the Christian theme of ecclesiology but through the critical lenses of postcolonialism.

Ecclesiology, in its simplest form, is the study of what it means to be 'church'. It is the examination of a body of people and their mission – a body, however, with problematic divisions. And from the outset the early Church sought out ways of transforming divisions in their ranks into the reality of Christ's body where there are no partitions (Gal. 3.27). However, the metaphor of the Church as a body has not erased differences; we have not all evolved into a new species devoid of problematic relationships of gender, class or ethnicity. So the struggle remains for the Church to offer signs of God's reign on earth. Specific to us is the question of how the black Pentecostal church tradition in Britain might better represent God's reign on earth.

Postcolonialism, as I understand it, is the recognition that, while the colonial period has ended, the world and indeed Christianity have not moved beyond the problems created by colonization. For this reason, former colonial subjects speak of neocolonialism, the idea that new forms of economic, political and military oppression replaced the old forms. Likewise, black British theorists talk of domestic neocolonialism to express the ways that the colonial order has been reconfigured in contemporary Britain. Applied to the Church, postcolonial theologians remind us that the weaving together of Christianity with commerce and racism led to complex relationships of domination and subordination, superiority and inferiority, between missionaries and their colonial converts. I am interested in colonial retention, specifically, the ways that the experience of slavery and colonization continue to impact on our ecclesiology, on what it means to be the people of God. To this end the title of this paper focuses our minds on how the *kerygma* (message) of the black Church, of African Caribbean origin, is muted by the continued impact of colonialism. Our ecclesiology, rather than being completely free from this past, is bound up with it in at least two ways: African retention and missionary retention.

African retention refers to the ways that slaves and colonial subjects adapted their traditional African beliefs to Christianity, so as to retain an African base or interpretation. A good example of this approach is found in Roswith Gerloff's study of the Oneness tradition in the 1980s and the emergence of the Church as a 'movement organization'.[3]

Missionary retention explores the ways that missionary theology was imposed upon African subjects and how this process continues to influence church life in the Caribbean and among its diaspora. A good example of this second school is Dianne Austin-Broos' study of Pentecostals in Jamaica. Broos focuses on the continued tension between the African rite or celebration and the missionary morality or moral orders. In reality the African Caribbean Christianity that informs black Pentecostalism in the UK is a mixture of the two, either an African adaptation of Christianity or a creolized mixture.

I am primarily interested in the second camp, missionary retention, but I want to approach it in a provocative way. I want to argue that we Pentecostals continue to live with the influence of missionary theology in many ways (including liturgy, doctrine and language). But I want to expose or 'out' other, often hidden, retentions related to the worst excesses of missionary theology – when missionary theology colludes with the rationality of racial terror and acts out this terror on black subjects as a form of occult practice.

I want to ask, 'Do we black Pentecostals live with the continued impact of a missionary bewitchment?' And, 'How might this continued bewitchment impact on our value of theological education?' When I refer to missionary bewitchment, I am thinking of corrupt Christian ideas and practices that can, through religious and anthropological studies, be considered occult.

There are four stages to this quest. First, I want to examine what we mean by bewitchment – the practice of witchcraft. Second, I want to apply a measure of what bewitchment is to the act of enslavement and missionary theology's legitimation of this terror. Next I want to explore the bicentennial of the abolition of the slave trade in Britain as an example of continued mass

bewitchment. And finally, I will examine how theological education or the lack of it continues to be influenced by bewitchment
tropes (themes).

Bewitchment

There is very little discussion of the nature of bewitchment in
the New Testament. Generally Satan and demonic forces are
understood to be the source of evil, and very little is said about
how demonic possession has taken place.[4] Given this silence,
I want to use African ideas of bewitchment as paradigmatic of
bewitchment.

Bewitchment is a concept I want to 'work' with but reverse the
popular African imagery. Rather than viewing it through pejora-
tive colonial lenses, I seek to decolonize and reverse it. I decolonize
it by thinking about it more universally and as a measure of occult
practices. I reverse its trajectory so that it is Western Christianity
rather than the belief system of native people that faces the
accusation of being the occult. This is not a completely new
idea in black religious studies. For some time, African American
religionist Charles H. Long has suggested that the religions of
enslaved and colonized peoples provide us with a view of the
coming of the West as a religious experience. For Long, the
coming of the West is signalled in the religions of colonized
peoples as the presence of a supernatural force or 'mysterium
tremendum'.[5] Neither is it a new idea in Caribbean religious
studies. Take, for instance, Jamaican religionist Dianne Stewart.
In her study Stewart examines a liberation or emancipation
motif running through African religions in Jamaica from slavery
through to Pentecostalism.[6] Implicit is a dialectical tension between
missionary Christianity and African religious retention: the former
corrupt and oppressive, and the latter providing solace, con-
tainment and even destruction of missionary religion. What this
suggests is that there is an African Jamaican interpretation of
slavery that was literal and spiritual.[7] Slavery was literal in that

the slaves encountered its physical brutality daily, but also spiritual in the sense that within their worldview such wrongdoing was a manifestation of evil. Importantly, the slaves' evaluation is not too different a conclusion of the essence of evil from that found in much of European Church history. Within Catholic Europe, the conceptualization of witchcraft was as a *reversal* of normal and socially accepted behaviour.[8]

I want to ground my understanding of bewitchment in the ideas contained in the slave world, where bewitchment is first and foremost a form of mystical violence. Mystical violence is related to a wider cosmological battle that pervades all of human life and all material objects. Within this schema, malignant or non-malignant forces, while invisible, have visible manifestation. The manifestation may be in putting individuals into a wrong state of mind as well as corrupting social relations. These two themes – the individual and structural impacts of mystical violence – allow us to navigate between the individual and society. This view has resonance with images of satanic oppression in the New Testament, where demonic forces possess and harass individuals such as Legion (Mark 5) as well as infecting systems and processes – what Paul calls 'elements of the world' in Galatians 4.3, 9.

While there is a vast range of scholarly opinion on the manifestation of malignant forces associated with witchcraft practices,[9] I want to work with one particular mode, that of the zombie and cannibal.

A zombie is a living dead person, and there is some evidence to show that this phenomenon originates in the African diaspora and is sent back to Africa as the result of inverted diasporic flow.[10] The zombie is a drone, experiencing a semi-human existence, and there are two contemporary manifestations. In South Africa, zombies are people who have been captured, bewitched and enslaved for the economic advantage of the bewitcher.[11] Similarly, but with a twist, in Haiti zombies are dead bodies brought back to life to function as economic slaves of their bewitchers.[12]

So, whether originating in life or death, the zombie is a living dead person, in a condition inextricably linked to the material enrichment of others. It is slavery, an ontological (being) captivity. Although the New Testament does not connect the demonic to the spirits of the dead, I believe that the image of the zombie has identification with the story of the Gerasene demoniac in Mark 5.1–15. Legion, after being healed, has a sound mind, suggesting to us that demonic oppression was a form of mental imbalance or a lack of sound mind. Furthermore Luke, by describing possession as enslavement to Satan (Acts 10.38), permits us to think of satanic possession or oppression as exploitation. So for me the zombie is in a possessed or oppressed state, one that results in an individual being in the wrong state of mind or having no mind and therefore being ripe for exploitation. As we shall see later, I will suggest that the zombie has diaspora identification with the Caribbean experience of mental slavery.

Cannibalism is deeply rooted in fears about the body and strangers: when you encounter different peoples, you fear for your body and think they will eat you.[13] As Victor Turner notes, cannibalism in Africa was reciprocal, both Africans and Europeans portraying each other as cannibals.[14] It is clear from historical records that European accusations were part of a process of dialectical othering designed to represent the Africans as primitive cannibals. But there was a very different understanding in African locations. As Comaroff and Comaroff note, cannibalism in colonial and modern Africa is linked to the experience of material and physical extraction.[15] When resources and people go missing, you interpret it through the language of cannibalism. Hence, the African accusation of cannibalism directed towards Europeans in the colonial period is related to the avaricious and rapacious consumption of Africans' resources as well as the capture and enslavement of their bodies. And it is this broader African perception that influences my thinking here. I want to think about cannibalism as an inappropriate consuming and devouring of the *other* – be that an economic, political, theological or cultural consumption – that devours all human productivity and reproduction. The idea of being devoured by a consuming and evil force is not alien to the New Testament. On the contrary, the image of the beast in Revelation 13 connotes rapacious activity akin to inappropriate devouring or cannibalism.

To review, there exists a great deal of variation in the actual mechanics of mystical violence, but we may speak of it as impacting one's being in the form of a zombie and also the consumption of essence in the form of the cannibal. Here, I want these perspectives on bewitchment practice, especially cannibalism, to represent a framework for understanding – themes to explain the nexus between missionary practice and contemporary Pentecostalism.

Next, I want to turn to the 'tipping point' – where Christian practice becomes a bewitching force.

Slavery and missionary Christianity as mystical violence

Traditionally, when theologians examine religion in relation to the slave world, we think in at least two ways: mission-centric and slave-centric. Mission-centric research refers to the normative gaze of the West: the bringing of Christianity by the missionaries as godly work to save the heathen from savagery. Slave-centric research refers to the counter-hegemonic response of slaves to missionary Christianity and their enslavement and, in particular, the adaptation of Christian thought to, or its syncretism with, indigenous African religions, explored through the modalities of survival, elevation and liberation.[16] I want to work within the second camp, but make my point of departure an assessment of Christianity as 'stronger magic' or mystical violence to be resisted.

We know that slaves understood their plight as more than economic and social; it was also a metaphysical attack. Two examples are useful to illustrate this fact. First, in Haiti the figure of the zombie is intimately related to the state of enslavement. According to anthropologist Mimi Sheller, in this modality the zombie reflects the fear of the return to slavery; its metabolic violence, lack of agency, and degrading slave labour.[17] She contemplates how one only needs to imagine powerless, dejected and broken slaves working in fields as forms of human drones devoid of personality to capture a sense of the zombie in Haiti's past.[18] Also, in *The Interesting Narrative of the Life of Olaudah Equiano, or Gustavus Vassa, the African* Olaudah Equiano notes his own and other captured slaves' interpretation of their plight as the result of bewitchment. For some, the blame lay with enemies in their village or among an opposing clan. For others, it was the newly encountered white strangers holding them captive in the 'factories on water' who had bewitched them and whom they feared would eat them.[19]

Now, I am not saying that all missionaries were bad or satanic; Caribbean history does not provide us with a simple dichotomy of good slaves and bad colonialists. However, the history does provide evidence of discursive formations, the organizing of material to produce particular representations and practices. In short, despite their best intentions for most of slave history in the Caribbean, missionaries were bound up with slavery's mystical violence.

As theologian James Perkinson reminds us, the question of the full humanity of Africans was always related to spirituality; that is, there was always metaphysics in mind.[20] The encounter of the sixteenth century was shaped by the dialectic of economics and faith. If Africans were equal to Europeans then they could be civilized, but equality provided *no* grounds for enslavement. So a regime of truth – a construction of values and beliefs enforced by power – marked and subjugated Africans as lesser beings. This way the dialectic was synthesized: Africans could be enslaved and Europeans' consciences salved by giving slaves Christian instruction. We know that initially the Catholic Church was against the idea of enslavement but soon conceded.[21] This was because evidence was provided to show that Africans were in need of civilizing: specifically, the missionary reports that Africans who resisted the gospel represented a rejection of Christ, and this rejection was seen as a sign of their carnality.[22] So Christianity went on to provide the justification or 'spell' for the sorcery of slavery with racialized readings of the biblical text.

The metaphysical question deteriorated into an all-out Christian assault on Africans, and it is at this point that Christianity becomes part of the occult, cursing and consuming Africans.

The curse or spell is taken from the 'Curse of Ham'. In Genesis 9, Noah's youngest son Ham has his son Canaan cursed as a result of Ham's refusal to cover his father's nakedness. This curse has an anti-black prehistory. It becomes associated with general slavery in the fourth-century writings of Augustine and takes on anti-blackness in medieval Talmudic texts.[23] By the sixteenth century it became a Christian theme and was fully accepted by the seventeenth as an explanation of black skin. Because black skin was divinely cursed, blacks could be consumed:

> European powers, in effect, 'ate' African substance in the slave trade (as well as 'native' substance in the colonial structures set up throughout the Americas, Asia and Pacific). Whatever the discourse, the fact of the effect is clear. A 'witchery' of heretofore unimaginable potency ravaged Africa and aboriginal cultures.[24]

Tragically, even after the abolition of slavery, legitimation of black inferiority was taken up by scientific inquiry, and, as sociologist Paul Gilroy notes in *Between Camps,* a new genomic racism stalks the planet, mobilizing science to justify continued subordination of African peoples.[25]

In sum, Christianity's complicity with enslavement and colonization implicates it with what Perkinson terms the West's 'witchery'. Seventeenth-century Christianity provided theological support (the curse), sanctioned zombification and cannibalism of black flesh, and participated in the orgy of violence – including the Church of England, which owned a slave plantation in Barbados.

But this was all such a long time ago and we have all moved on? Right? After all, didn't we have a ceremony in 2007 where the powerful and good met to celebrate Wilberforce's abolition of the slave trade? I think not. This leads to my third point, that the remnants of bewitchment, particularly zombism, are very much with us in the present.

Remnants of bewitchment

African Caribbean Christianity is a healing tradition. Historically a product of both African and European sources, our tradition has consistently sought to make whole black bodies and psyches through the good news of Jesus Christ, the Son of God. Central to this task is worship, where the seeker or believer encounters God in power and holiness and is transformed into a new creature and new creation, as a result of being filled with the Holy Spirit. At its best, African Caribbean Christianity is one of the greatest examples of individual transformation. We have perfected making nobody somebody or, as Anthony Pinn would say, moving individuals from fixed objectivity to complex subjectivity.[26] The founder of Western Pentecostalism, William Seymour, understood the power of faith to transform black life, individually and structurally. For Seymour, tongues were a language of equality.[27] This is why the church at Azusa initially sought to break down barriers of race, class and gender. You could not have tongues and continue with oppression. Azusa was on one level a form of exorcism of destructive social relationships and an end to separatism – a form of structural support for the economic cannibalism of American apartheid. But I want to suggest that today in the UK we still need deliverance from missionary bewitchment.

I want to propose that there exist contemporary manifestations of bewitchment. This is the beginning of a process of identifying historical relationships that I do not have sufficient time to explore in depth here. But for now I want to suggest that there are continued forms of devouring associated with the fear of politics.

Fear of politics refers to the way that rampant eschatology (focus on the afterlife) secured slave obedience and passivity in the present. In short, a particular theology facilitated the continued devouring of the colonial state. Today this theme is played out in a hermeneutic that produces spiritual readings of the text rather than engagement with social justice. Now, I know that a great deal of work has been completed over the past decade to identify the social work carried out by members of black churches and their occasional foray into political arenas. But the most recent study by Berrisford Lewis reveals that black church social engagement is mostly reactive and piecemeal, and that politics is still marginal to church life.[28] The fear of political engagement leaves us vulnerable to exploitation and brutalization – cannibalistic forces. The failure to reckon with the fear of politics produces a modern form of cannibalism that limits the ability of black Pentecostals to engage with the social world and fight against the multivalent forms of devouring impacting on black communities.

Case study of cannibalism: the bicentennial

Now, I am sure that there are some people here who are convinced that my arguments don't add up as there is no case of black Christians being devoured by neo-cannibalistic forces in the UK. So to end, I want to present a case study of mass black Pentecostal devouring in the Westminster Abbey service that was part of the 2007 bicentennial of the abolition of the slave trade in Britain. Let's begin with the background.

The bicentennial of the abolition of the British transatlantic slave trade set out to commemorate, if not cryptically 'celebrate', the work of the abolitionist movement. Foregrounding the abolitionist William Wilberforce, a multitude of events were organized. However, a heated debate ensued on how best to reflect on the history from a variety of contemporary locations. A great deal of debate circulated around whether the nation should give an apology for its unjust enrichment from slavery. In the end 'deep regret' was expressed by the UK government, although some of the cities with slaving in their past (the cities of Liverpool and London) went further and provided municipal government-led apologies. Bristol, a city steeped in slavery, flatly refused to offer any meaningful statement of apology or serious regret, much to the annoyance of the bicentennial event's organizers and activists. The religious focal point of the commemoration was a high-profile British establishment service led by the Archbishop of Canterbury, Rowan Williams, at Westminster Abbey in London.

The service will be remembered for Pan-Africanist Toyin Agbetu's dramatic and solitary protest in front of Queen Elizabeth II and the then UK prime minister, Tony Blair. But I want to suggest that the real 'offence' was the inability of the service to reckon with and atone for Christian complicity in enslavement; as a result, rather than challenging a history of collusion, it simply reinforced a particular form of black zombification, that is, epistemic violence – imposition of one way of doing things that belittles and deceives the other.

Let us recap the protest. About 45 minutes into the commemoration at Westminster Abbey, Mr Agbetu began screaming at the top of his voice, while the Queen, Prince Philip, Tony and Cherie Blair and the Archbishop of Canterbury watched in disbelief. Intriguingly, his protest began just as the archbishop had delivered his main address and the service had moved on to 'confession and absolution'. At that point Agbetu shouted, 'You should be ashamed! We should not be here. This is an insult to us. I want all the Christians who are Africans to walk out of here with me!' No one got up to follow him. In fact, most of the black people were as bemused as the members of the ruling class; others fixed their faces like stone to signify shame and disgust.

I watched the events unfold on the BBC World Service in my hotel room in Accra (I was in Ghana filming a documentary on the underside of globalization) and my first thought was whether or not the protester would get out of there alive. After all, in this supposedly terrorist-conscious era people get shot for *looking* like a terrorist, much less acting like one. The fears of the security guards were eased somewhat when he yelled, 'I have no weapon! I have no weapon!' Later on, it became clear that this protest was pre-planned, as Mr Agbetu stated afterwards: 'I don't believe it was right for us to have remained in a venue in which the British monarchy, government and church – all leading institutions of African enslavement during the Maafa – collectively refused to atone for their sins.'[29]

There are two possible reasons for the protest. First, Agbetu's contention circulates around the question of participation of black people in the absurd. He erupted at the point of the prayer for confession and forgiveness; strangely enough, the preamble to this was read by Pastor Agu, a senior pastor for Redeemed Church of God, a diaspora Nigerian congregation. If the black people were specifically being asked to recognize and forgive African complicity, that is understandable. But if, as Mr Agbetu and many others within the abbey seemed to think, they were being asked to forgive an event in which their ancestors were victims, the lack of mass action and protest intrigues me.

The second issue is the more perplexing question of an apology. There was no state or Church apology at the service, and when the dean led the congregation into the confessional prayer there was very little clarity as to who was praying for what, although we should note that Prime Minister Blair and the archbishop made a statement of deep regret, and had apologized previously for the involvement of state and Church respectively. State regret and Church apology went some way towards reducing the pressure on the Queen to apologize for the nation's past sin and continued benefit from slavery's genocide. This may be why the demand by a senior member of the Anglican Communion for a public act of penance by the Queen was quickly dismissed by the event's organizers.

So how do we explain this strange theological occurrence at the abbey?

One explanation for the clumsy liturgy lies with the limitations of atonement theology. Atonement theology is a complex tradition of thought and action, focusing on the reasons for the death of Christ. The atoning work of Christ is re-enacted in Christian liturgy through the recognition of wrongdoing and the forgiveness of sins – making the individual and the congregation 'right' with God and each other. In fact, the theme of reconciliation is 'shot through' the theory and practice of atonement. In recent years black and liberation theologians have acknowledged that the traditional atonement models, while enabling the subject to atone for private guilt and personal wrongdoing, do not sufficiently address corporate or structural evil and wrongdoing. In contrast, atonement theories from 'the underside' broaden the scope of salvation to encompass the individual and the social. Liberation theologian Gustavo Gutierrez explains it this way: 'In the liberation approach sin is not considered as an individual, private, or merely interior reality'; instead, 'sin is regarded as a social, historical fact'.[30]

Consequently the liberation vision of the atoning work of Christ demands right relationship between individuals and the destruction of oppressive structures, systems and practices that limit or destroy the promise of life to the full. Naturally, Agbetu, as part of the reparations movement, would affirm a more demanding approach that recognizes national complicity and culpability in the unjust gain of slavery – that is, *structural* sin. Structural sin acknowledges that evil can be systemic, a 'domination system' that is manifested in unjust social and political systems, within institutions as well as personal action. Awareness of structural sin facilitates a refocusing on how unjust historical processes have resulted in unjust enrichment and the pain and suffering of others.

But another explanation is the persistence of derivations of mystical violence, specifically epistemic violence or brutalizing knowledge aimed at servitude. I think that Agbetu seems to have realized what very few Christians within the abbey were aware of – that they were experiencing a process as old as the colonies themselves, that is, a form of devouring in the form of epistemic or knowledge violence, where ideas and worldviews and *control of memory* inflict a mental damage that has the same brutalizing role as whips and chains did during Caribbean slavery. Let me explain.

Epistemic violence

I want to suggest that epistemic violence is modern-day devouring. To understand it this way we must recognize that two important marks of slave servitude were re-enacted at Westminster Abbey. To describe these marks of servitude, I want to work with the argument of Jamaican sociologist Orlando Patterson, who states that slavery was enforced through *symbol and ritual and incorporated one or more of four basic features*:

> First the symbolic rejection of the slave of his past, and his former kinsmen; second a change of name; third the imposition of some visible mark of servitude; and last, the assumption of a new status in the household or economic organization of the master.[31]

I believe that all four marks of enforcing slavery or, as he terms it, 'social death' were present in the abbey service.

The first act of remaking is removing or distorting the memory of the slave. As Patterson states: 'Many cultures obliged the new slave to make a symbolic gesture of rejecting his natal community, kinsmen, ancestral spirits and gods . . .'[32]

Generally speaking, much of the commemorative year was an attack on the appropriate memory. As systematic theologian Miroslav Volf informs us, appropriate Christian memory is that which brings about healing in the present. Instead we received an ideological representation of the slave past and the British Empire's role within it. A Wilberforceization ensured that less attention was paid to slave revolts or African abolitionists. For instance, the media marginalized Caribbean analysis, which places the emphasis for abolition on economic forces, slave revolts and changes in production rather than on British benevolence. Also a national selective historical amnesia failed to relate the fact that 1807 meant very little to Africans or those enslaved in the 'West Indies' as it took another 30 years before the semblance of freedom emerged. Even then, following formal emancipation in 1834, the sugar plantations were productively worked by schemes of indentured labour. The foregrounding of a particular vision of William Wilberforce within the abbey service and the marginalization of real historical consequences is, I believe, coded liturgical enforcement of a distortion of memory.

Second, slavery was also concerned with some visible mark of servitude. As Patterson notes, 'in such large scale systems this task was performed by state religion.'[33] A central ideological force for maintaining social, cultural and political hegemony during British West Indian slavery was religion. English Christian religion was reworked in the Caribbean to accommodate the *Maafa*. Initially very little attempt was made to take Christianity to the enslaved. The plantation class feared that conversion would mean equality and therefore a loss of 'stock', and resisted interference from the Church in legal or civil matters. But lack of planter support was exacerbated by a general apathy from the Anglican Church towards colonial mission. Most of the early priests who did venture to the West Indian colonies were more bent on their own material gain than on evangelization – even among the planter class and poor whites. So for at least 150 years West Indians 'lived as heathens in the so-called parishes'.[34] However, the situation was eased when the Church was able to reassure planters that the soteriological distinction between the status of the African slave and the European in the divine plan made it possible, if not desirable, to enslave these so-called lesser breeds before God. Within this scheme, the Bible was interpreted not as a book of liberation but as a book of law and judgement to govern slave behaviour,[35] encouraging slaves to fear spiritual sin and opt for 'divine enslavement'.[36] I am suggesting that the passivity of black Christians at the abbey signifies a mark of continued servitude to the mastery and superiority of Western Christianity.

The brutalization of memory and capitulation to Western theology, for me, represents continued mystical violence, a devouring represented in the form of epistemic violence. Having spoken to some of those present, it was clear that there was a range of responses to the bicentennial service. There was a real sense of confusion and spiritual conflict over the trajectory of the liturgy. But only one person, a non-Christian, protested.

Conclusion

The 'bewitchment' theme provides us with a focus for revising and re-visioning the mission of the Church. To look outwards we must also look inwards. In other words we need to move from maintaining things to a new mission. Central to this quest is the need to address the derivations of mystical violence that continue to haunt us in an unwillingness to engage with political matters. But the service at Westminster Abbey leads to another continued influence: epistemic violence. So, in conclusion, I argue for an exorcism on two levels.

First, there is a need for an exorcism of the fear of politics. We must develop a meaningful political theory and political presence both locally and nationally. Politics is fundamentally concerned with the negotiation of power. How can those of us committed to renouncing power transform a world bent on getting as much of it as possible? I believe we need to think deeply and courageously to develop new ways of mirroring the egalitarian, counter-cultural values of the kingdom of God and to seek out ways of making these resources the basis for social transformation. That is, *if* your church believes in the equality of all before God, be they men or women, Caribbean or African, young or old.

Second, exorcism of our susceptibility to epistemic violence must come in the form of a radical commitment to serious theological education. Tragically, with only less than 1 per cent of black Pentecostal clergy possessing university degrees in theology, we are currently one of the least theologically qualified sections of Christendom worldwide, if not the least. Put succinctly, exorcism must address black Pentecostal theological solipsism or the institutionalization of ignorance, its greatest manifestation being the poor quality of biblical exegesis and preaching: not so much ministry as minstrelsy. Moving from maintenance to mission is, on one level, an act of exorcism.

Notes

1 James Cone, lecture at Queen's College, Birmingham, 1996.

2 Robert Beckford, *Jesus Dub: Theology, Music and Social Change*, London: Routledge, 2006; Robert Beckford, *Documentary as Exorcism: Resisting the Bewitchment of Colonial Christianity*, London and New York: Continuum, 2013.

3 Roswith Gerloff, *A Plea for British Black Theologies: The Black Church Movement in Britain in Its Transatlantic Cultural and Theological Interaction*, vol. 1, Frankfurt and New York: Peter Lang, 1992.

4 E. Sorensen, *Possession and Exorcism in the New Testament and Early Christianity*, Tübingen: J. C. Mohr, 2002, pp. 1–5; K. Warrington, *Pentecostal Theology: A Theology of Encounter*, London: Continuum, 2008, pp. 293–300.

5 C. H. Long, *Significations*, Minneapolis: Fortress Press, 1986, p. 9.

6 Dianne M. Stewart, *Three Eyes for the Journey: African Dimensions of the Jamaican Religious Experience*, Oxford: Oxford University Press, 2005.

7 Stewart, *Three Eyes*, pp. 189–241.

8 James L. Brain, 'An Anthropological Perspective on the Witchcraze', in Arthur C. Lehmann et al., *Magic, Witchcraft and Religion: An Anthropological Study of the Supernatural*, 6th edn, Boston: McGraw-Hill, 2005.

9 M. Gaskill, *Witchcraft: A Very Short Introduction*, Oxford: Oxford University Press, 2010; J. Comaroff and J. L. Comaroff, 'Introduction',

in J. Comaroff and J. L. Comaroff (eds), *Modernity and Its Malcontents: Ritual and Power in Postcolonial Africa*, Chicago: University of Chicago Press, 1993.

10 Peter Geschiere, *The Modernity of Witchcraft, Politics, and the Occult in Postcolonial Africa*, Charlottesville, VA and London: University of Virginia Press, 1997.

11 Isak Niehaus et al., *Witchcraft, Power and Politics*, London: Pluto Press, 1993.

12 Karen McCarthy Brown, 'Voodoo', in Arthur C. Lehmann et al., *Magic, Witchcraft, and Religion: An Anthropological Study of the Supernatural*, 6th edn, Boston: McGraw-Hill, 2005, p. 321.

13 Mary Douglas, *Purity and Danger: An Analysis of the Concepts of Pollution and Taboo*, New York: Praeger, 1966.

14 Victor Turner, *Schism and Continuity in African Society*, Oxford: Berg, 1996, p. 23.

15 Comaroff and Comaroff, 'Introduction', in Comaroff and Comaroff (eds), *Modernity and Its Malcontents*.

16 See, for example, Anthony Pinn, *Terror and Triumph: The Meaning of Black Religion*, Minneapolis: Fortress Press, 2003, pp. 81–156.

17 M. Sheller, *Consuming the Caribbean: From Arawaks to Zombies*, London: Routledge, 2003, p. 145.

18 Sheller, *Consuming*, p. 145.

19 Olaudah Equiano, *The Interesting Narrative and Other Writings* (ed. Vincent Carretta), London: Penguin, 1995, p. 55.

20 James W. Perkinson, *White Theology: Outing Supremacy in Modernity*, New York: Palgrave Macmillan, 2004, p. 35.

21 Daniel Castro, *Another Face of Empire: Bartolomé de las Casas, Indigenous Rights, and Ecclesiastical Imperialism*, Durham, NC: Duke University Press, 2007.

22 See A. Loomba and J. Burton (eds), *Race in Early Modern England: A Documentary Companion*, London: Palgrave Macmillan, 2007.

23 David M. Goldenberg, *The Curse of Ham: Race and Slavery in Early Judaism, Christianity and Islam*, Princeton: Princeton University Press, 2005.

24 James W. Perkinson, *Shamanism, Racism, and Hip-Hop Culture: Essays on White Supremacy and Black Subversion*, New York: Palgrave Macmillan, 2005, p. 26.

25 Paul Gilroy, *Between Camps: Nations, Cultures and the Allure of Race*, London: Allen Lane, 2000.
26 Pinn, *Terror and Triumph*, p. 105.
27 Robert Beckford, *God of the Rahtid: Redeeming Rage*, London: Darton, Longman and Todd, 2003.
28 Berrisford Lewis, 'African-Caribbean Pentecostal Church Leaders and Socio-Political Engagement in Contemporary Britain', unpublished PhD thesis, University of Birmingham, 2008.
29 *The Guardian*, 3 April 2007.
30 Gustavo Gutierrez, *A Theology of Liberation*, London: SCM Press, 1974, p. 24.
31 Orlando Patterson, *Slavery and Social Death: A Comparative Study*, Cambridge, MA: Harvard University Press, 1982, p. 54.
32 Patterson, *Slavery*, p. 54.
33 Patterson, *Slavery*, p. 54.
34 Keith Hunter, 'Protestantism and Slavery in the British Caribbean', in Armando Lampe, *Christianity in the Caribbean*, Barbados, Jamaica, Trinidad and Tobago: University of the West Indies Press, 2001, p. 89.
35 Patterson, *Slavery*, p. 54.
36 Patterson, *Slavery*, p. 71.

3

Pentecostal hermeneutics

RUTHLYN BRADSHAW

Introduction

Being invited to contribute to this lecture series is indeed an honour and I thank you. It is highly commendable that we have been afforded this forum to come together and reflect theologically about our faith. The contributions made by the two previous contributors were excellent, informative and thought-provoking. I sincerely hope that my contribution will be a continuation of the high standard that has already been set.

Our discussion today is based on the theme, 'Pentecostal hermeneutics', which is quite a large and extensive theological theme. It is impossible to cover it or even do it justice in a single lecture. However, by presenting some of the issues, I trust that our curiosities will be sufficiently aroused to inspire further exploration of the subject.

Pentecostalism

Pentecostalism, as we know it, is a little over a century old and is estimated to be the fastest-growing movement within Christianity today. I am sure that the early pioneers did not foresee or even imagine that the revival which started in 1906 in a rundown mission on Azusa Street, Los Angeles, California, under the ministry of the black preacher William Seymour, would have resulted in a movement drawing millions of adherents.

It is important to note that there were other manifestations of Holy Spirit baptisms with speaking in tongues predating the Azusa Revival. One such incidence occurred in a prayer meeting on

1 January 1901, when students in Charles Fox Parham's Bible school in Topeka, Kansas, received the baptism of the Holy Spirit and began speaking in tongues. Parham's identification in Scripture that speaking in tongues is the Bible evidence, or 'initial evidence' as it was later called, of Spirit baptism became a defining mark of the emerging Pentecostal movement.[1] However, the Apostolic Faith movement under Parham's leadership remained confined to the south-central United States, while the revival at Azusa Street propelled Pentecostalism before a worldwide audience. It is generally agreed that the existing worldwide Pentecostal movements have been in part the outgrowth of the ministry of the African American preacher William Seymour and the Azusa Street Revival.

Seymour was not only a preacher but also an advocate for human rights and justice. Confronted by the many critics and social factors of his time, he became the initiator of a multiracial worshipping community. He preached racial reconciliation and equality. A situation where blacks and whites worshipped together under a black pastor, at a time when racism and segregation were at their peak, was truly an incredible and momentous achievement. Seymour, going against the status quo, also rejected the barriers that were erected to keep women out of church leadership. It is reported that seven of the twelve elders in the Azusa Street Mission were women. It is also recorded that women were instrumental in spreading the Pentecostal message far beyond the region of Los Angeles.

Early Pentecostal believers were fuelled by their beliefs and understanding of the events which occurred in the book of Acts. They were convinced that the baptism in the Holy Spirit, with the immediate accompaniment of speaking in tongues and the manifestations of the Spirit, did not end with the book of Acts, but is available to believers in all ages. They firmly grasped and believed Peter's statement:

> Repent, and be baptized every one of you in the name of Jesus Christ for the remission of sins, and ye shall receive the gift of the Holy Ghost. For the promise is unto you, and to your children, and to all that are afar off, even as many as the LORD our God shall call. (Acts 2.38–39 KJV)

Those who claimed to have received the baptism in the Holy Spirit testified to having a greater awareness and overwhelming sense of the presence of God; an experience which totally rejuvenated and reordered their lives.

Defining Pentecostalism is almost an impossible task, as many before have attested. Pentecostalism has been and still is the subject of numerous studies and research. In his book, *Pentecostal Theology*, Keith Warrington has pointed out, through the use of several quotations, the difficulties and challenges which have confronted scholars and writers in their attempts to define and 'identify the heartbeat of Pentecostalism'.[2]

Pentecostalism refers to a wide variety of movements, brought about by doctrinal differences resulting in divisions and formations of numerous organizations with political, social and theological differences. There are three strands of Pentecostalism that I will mention here. The first strand consists of the Classical Pentecostals, referring to those Christians active in churches that are readily identified as Pentecostals. They believe in conversion followed by Holy Spirit baptism accompanied by speaking in tongues. This is the group referred to throughout this lecture. The second strand is represented by the Oneness Pentecostals. They have a non-Trinitarian understanding of God. The third strand is made up of the Neo-Pentecostals: those who come from a wide variety of theological backgrounds and have remained in their respective church traditions. They have 'attempted to reconcile the Pentecostal dimensions of their religious experience with the theological deposit of their respective traditions'.[3] Father Dennis Bennett, an Episcopal minister, confessed from his pulpit that 'the Holy Spirit did take my lips and tongue and form a new and powerful language of praise and prayer that I myself could not understand'.[4] Pentecostalism is very diverse, yet held together by a common shared experience and similar emphasis on the Holy Spirit and Spirit manifestations.

Pentecostals and theology

Pentecostal beliefs have given rise to much speculation, mis-understanding and criticism. One of the common criticisms of the Pentecostal movement is its lack of an adequate theology. 'Popular portrayals of Pentecostalism often imply that theology is virtu-ally absent from this movement.'[5] Pentecostals have been known to suffer from a deficiency in the theology and teaching depart-ment. Walter Hollenweger, a former Pentecostal, reveals this when he writes the following dedication: 'To my friends and teachers in the Pentecostal Movement who taught me to love the Bible and to my teachers and friends in the Presbyterian Church who taught me to understand it.'[6] Although not a totally true statement, it has often been said that Pentecostals engage their hearts (emotions) rather than their minds.

However, it is an undeniable fact that in some instances, espe-cially in the earlier years, Pentecostals have shied away from formal theological studies and training. Dr Joe Aldred in his lecture diagnosed the condition as theology-phobia and suggests that it's time for us to get rid of it. In recent times, thank God, there is evidence of change. Pentecostal theologians and adequately trained Pentecostal ministers are emerging, individuals who are no longer content with 'just opening their mouths wide and waiting for God to fill them'. That being said, there is still much work to be done as residues from the old way of thinking still remain with us. Just a few months ago I was told by a well-meaning Pentecostal, 'You'd better rely on the Holy Ghost and stop studying all that theology stuff or you're going to lose the anointing.' Obviously, some Chris-tians are misguided and misinformed as to what theology is.

'Theology is the study of God, his attributes, and his relation-ship with man and the universe.'[7] Theology seeks to understand by reaching below the surface of life, trying to gain deeper under-standing of God, of his being, nature and relationship with the world. It asks questions such as: What is God like? What does God do? How does God treat us? No thinking, reflecting Christian can escape doing theology; whether knowingly or unknowingly, we are all engaged in doing theology. As a matter of fact, an authentic Christian faith will lead a person towards wanting to understand the God who has such claims upon his or her life. As Pentecostals we must move beyond just stating truths to examining and exploring the significance of our beliefs, our teachings and our faith assertions. Black American theologian James Cone said, 'theology is the critical side of the faith, and without it faith loses its distinctive identity.'[8] It would be helpful if theological reflection was encouraged in Pentecostal churches, providing members with the space and the opportunity to explore and think theologically about their faith.

Pentecostal theology

Pentecostal theology has been influenced by many theological traditions. In order to understand Pentecostal hermeneutics, some considerations must be given to its theological roots. Classical Pentecostalism emerged mainly from the Wesleyan and Holiness movements. According to *The Dictionary of Pentecostal and Charismatic Movements*, 'the hermeneutical tendencies of eighteenth-century preacher and theologian John Wesley bear tremendous implications for the study of Pentecostal hermeneutics.'[9] It notes four dominating hermeneutical principles coming out of Wesley's work. First, Wesley loved Scripture, read it at length and embraced it with 'a passion so consuming that it transformed his very pattern of speech'.[10] Second, Bible study for him was not simply an academic exercise but 'a devotional experience'.[11] Third, he regarded the Bible as an authoritative source of doctrine. And finally, he saw the application of the biblical message as a necessary conclusion.

The Holiness movement also decisively influenced Pentecostal hermeneutics and theology. Its teachings on the baptism of the Holy Spirit subsequent to regeneration provided the groundwork upon which the Pentecostal theology of Spirit baptism after conversion could later be built.

Pentecostalism has often been characterized by speaking in tongues, as if that was its only ingredient. David du Plessis explained that Pentecostal fervour and vibrancy were not 'because we speak with tongues, for if that was all we had from the experience ... we would have been a forgotten issue long ago'.[12] Anderson also pointed out that 'Early Pentecostals did not consider speaking in tongues the message of the movement, but rather a means by which the message was confirmed, legitimized and propagated. The message was "Jesus is coming soon." '[13] That was the main thrust of early Pentecostal theology, and everything experienced was in keeping with this. An 'eschatological intensity' and 'existential identification' with the 'full gospel message' of New Testament apostolic Christianity[14] all helped to shape Pentecostals. Pentecostal theology is a functional theology that exists to operate, exploring beliefs in the context of praxis.

Pentecostals possess an implicit though not explicit theology of the Spirit which places strong emphasis on the role of the Spirit in the life of the believer and in the Church. Spirit baptism with the 'initial evidence' of speaking in tongues, the manifestations of the gifts of the Spirit, the fruit of the Spirit, divine healing and the imminent return of the Lord Jesus are all part of Pentecostal theology. Pentecostals are Spirit-driven, 'Spirit conscious, Spirit filled and Spirit empowered believers',[15] possessing an experiential 'living faith in a living God'.[16]

Pentecostals and the Bible

The following three quotations affirm the importance of the Bible to Pentecostals: 'The Pentecostals were a people of "the book", avidly reading it over and over in a crudely literal manner.'[17] '[A] cardinal principle of Pentecostalism has always been strict adherence first and foremost to the Bible.'[18] '[T]he full Gospel message was birthed as marginalized Christian peoples from the Anglo and African slave Holiness communities read Scripture with revivalistic restorative lenses.'[19]

Pentecostals hold fast to the traditional evangelical position that Scripture is the divinely revealed word of God, the only authoritative rule for faith and practice, and to the infallibility of the Scriptures. According to Frederick Bruner, 'Pentecostalism quite openly declares that unless it can support its case biblically, it has no finally compelling reason to exist.'[20] As stated in the *Pentecostal and Charismatic Dictionary*, Pentecostals affirm the infallibility of the Bible while recognizing that 'they have neither the ability nor responsibility to demonstrate this infallibility . . . [Since] the Bible is inspired by an infallible God, it is infallible. No further demonstration of its infallibility is either necessary or possible.'[21]

Pentecostals have a unique approach to Scripture. They 'read the Bible as a presently inspired story'.[22] They come to the text knowing that the word of God transcends mere human ability to interpret it: 'the natural man receiveth not the things of the Spirit of God: for they are foolishness unto him: neither can he know them, because they are spiritually discerned' (1 Cor. 2.14 KJV). They depend on the Holy Spirit for inspiration and illumination and also to bridge the gap between then and now, the ancient text and today. This brings us to the question of hermeneutics.

Hermeneutics

Pentecostal hermeneutics has often come under fire. Gordon Fee says that Pentecostals are 'noted for bad hermeneutics',[23] and that 'hermeneutics has simply not been a Pentecostal thing'.[24] I am tempted to agree with him after some of the statements I have heard from several black Pentecostals on the subject. I was left with the impression that many don't know and are not very interested in knowing about the hermeneutical or theological aspects of their tradition. One told me emphatically, 'God said it, I believe it and that settles it.' That's noble and good, but is it enough? How do we know what God said or is saying?

Hermeneutics is the art or the science of interpretation, especially of scriptural text. It is about discovering meaning in the Bible for our lives and our times. Most religious traditions basically follow a similar set of hermeneutical principles; for example: the priority of the biblical language, historical context, accommodation of revelation and principles applying to the various genres found in the biblical literature such as poetry, history, letter, law and so on. However, while Pentecostals share certain basic presuppositions with other evangelicals concerning Scripture, they also have some distinctive ones.

From the outset,

> Pentecostals have understood that scriptures can be interpreted properly only through the agency of the Holy Spirit. Convinced of the importance of the Holy Spirit to the interpreting process, they bear a distinct witness to an experience and life in the Spirit, out of which Pentecostal hermeneutics and theology have emerged.[25]

Pentecostal hermeneutics is not only informed by the experience of salvation, but also by their baptism in the Holy Spirit and how this affects their lives.

The hermeneutical task cannot be done independently of ourselves. One must be cognizant of the fact that 'no one interprets in a theological vacuum'.[26] Regardless of one's religious persuasion, every interpreter brings to the process of interpretation many embedded theological presuppositions. Tradition, culture, experiences and worldview are all factors which come into play when interpreting the Scriptures. Pentecostal hermeneutics 'incorporates different but legitimate methodological, personal, historical, and theological presupposition in its interpretive work'.[27] Each interpreter brings to the process of interpretation intentionally or unintentionally his or her personal experiences.

The lens through which we read the text will have tremendous influence upon our hermeneutics. Pentecostal hermeneutics incorporates an experiential dimension, bringing to the text experiential presupposition. Experience gives an important pre-understanding of the text. It is only natural that Pentecostals will bring their experience of Holy Spirit baptism to the book of Acts. The person who is baptized in the Holy Spirit, with the evidence of speaking in tongues, will understand better what tongue-speaking is and will relate more easily to the account in Acts than the person who has never spoken in tongues. The same goes for someone who has experienced conversion or healing: his or her understanding of the accounts of conversion and healing in the Bible will be better than that of someone who has no such experience.

Pentecostals approach Scripture with a supernatural expectancy, believing God can and will act supernaturally now as he did in the past. If God did it for people in Bible days, he will do it for them now. They are sensitive not only to the text but to the promise contained in them. They read with an eye not only to the past but also to the present and the future, making meaningful connections. They read through a lens of expectancy, seeing God's actions as continuous, acting today towards the same purposes, and ask, 'What is God doing now and how do I fit into it?'

Common criticisms of Pentecostal hermeneutics

Pentecostal hermeneutics has come under criticism for several reasons.

The Pentecostal experience

Fee argues that 'Pentecostals' experience has preceded their hermeneutics. In a sense, the Pentecostal tends to exegete his or her experience'.[28] Fee's argument is based on the fact that the doctrine of Holy Spirit baptism, subsequent to salvation, did not flow out of a Pentecostal reading of the Scripture, but when Pentecostals did have the experience of the Spirit after conversion, this helped them to see a pattern in the Scriptures, which they then used to support their own experience and 'made it normative for all Christians'.[29] Pentecostals are not denying that the initial experience did precede the theological formation, but does that lessen or discredit the experience or invalidate their interpretation of it? Has personal experience of the baptism of the Holy Spirit aided or impeded Pentecostal interpretation of Scripture? If the experience of Spirit baptism is from God, then the experience itself should only help the interpretation. Isn't Scripture one long record of people's experiences of God?

Scripture versus experience

Pentecostals have been accused of putting personal experience above Scripture. It is believed by critics that experience is allowed to carry too much weight in interpretation and Scripture is then understood in the light of experience, rather than the other way around. But is there such a thing as total objectivity and impersonal exegesis? Anderson explains that Pentecostals

> are willing to admit that their understanding of Scripture is formed, in part, by what they have experienced. This does not elevate experience above the text. It simply means that as an expression of Christianity which emphasizes and appreciates the personal . . . dimension of a relationship with God, Pentecostals rather unabashedly admit they reflect upon their own experiences as they study the text.[30]

As previously stated, we all come to Scripture with presuppositions which take in all of our previous experiences. At least Pentecostals are willing to admit this.

Hermeneutic deficiency

Pentecostals have no developed hermeneutics. Fee said,

> Their attitude towards Scripture regularly has included a general disregard for scientific exegesis and carefully thought-out hermeneutics. Scripture is the Word of God and is to be obeyed. In place of scientific hermeneutics there developed a kind of pragmatic hermeneutics – obey what should be taken literally; spiritualize, allegorize, or devotionalize the rest.[31]

It is what it is

Another argument is that Pentecostals' appeal to the Spirit insulates their interpretations from correction. Some claim that the Holy

Spirit directly told them or gave them the interpretation and meaning. This can give rise to erroneous doctrines and weird interpretations. How does one correct the Spirit?

Pentecostals admit the possibility of abuse, but in spite of that, it cannot be ruled out that the Spirit can give an awareness of meaning. They acknowledge that the Holy Spirit works through the Scriptures and never against them, and dependence on the Holy Spirit does not allow one to interpret Scripture in isolation.

Holier than thou

It is thought that Pentecostals portray a kind of spiritual elitism in their hermeneutics. Their emphasis on the pneumatic and on baptism in the Holy Spirit makes it appear as if they have a better vantage point, an insight and understanding which is unavailable to non-Pentecostals. Well?

Shaky foundation

Pentecostals are accused of having no real hermeneutical base to support one of their greatest claims. Frank Farrell claims that 'the few historical accounts in Acts, in comparison with other Scriptures, provide a flimsy foundation indeed upon which to erect a doctrine of Christian life'.[32] Theological truths cannot be reduced to numerical frequency. If that be the case why do we embrace other major theological truths with limited occurrences in Scripture? An example of this is the virgin birth.

Pentecostal hermeneutics may be different but is it legitimate? Is there only one sound method for doing hermeneutics? Is there a method for doing hermeneutics that eliminates error completely? Pentecostals do not boast of an infallible hermeneutical method; while they rely strongly on the Holy Spirit for guidance, humans ultimately do the interpretation. Interpretation, therefore, is susceptible to error and will always have the possibility of error associated with it. Our discernments are bound by our imperfections.

We admit that there are elements in Pentecostal hermeneutics that subject it to all sorts of abuse. Pentecostals must employ every means possible to preserve what is valid and useful and be ruthless enough to oppose all that is erroneous. Pentecostals do not have licence or free rein to interpret Scripture irresponsibly, but must respect the generally accepted hermeneutical principles such as paying attention to the historical (what it meant when it was written), canonical (treating the Bible as a whole document), symbolic–allegorical (what is represented) and rational (thinking it through, using logic and deductive techniques). Also the interpreter 'must give proper recognition to both the divine and human elements that coexist in the scriptures . . . these two facets of the nature of scripture must be held in constant tension in order to avoid hermeneutical excess'.[33] Furthermore, we should be committed to serious sober study by engaging the mind as well as the heart.

'Black' Pentecostal churches: stewards of a great heritage

We are recipients of a great heritage. From the beginning, William Seymour, filled with the Holy Spirit and driven with the desire for equality and justice, made a difference by changing the existing order of things. Effecting change was an integral part of the Pentecostal experience right from the start. People of all classes, races and genders were given a new sense of identity and significance. The Pentecostal Church was a force for change. The disciples, filled with the Holy Spirit, went forth from the upper room and turned the world upside down. How are we bearing witness to this heritage? Where are we doing battle for justice? Where are the evidences that we are effecting change? How are we liberating people from an oppressive society?

Black Pentecostal churches in the UK are not here by chance or by mere human initiatives, as we all know. However we came about or got started, it was God who orchestrated it and strategically set us in place for the continuation of the Pentecostal mission and message. Back in the early twentieth century it was the Church that kept black people going, and the Church must keep black people going now.

'The Pentecostal Movement was formed from the margins of mainstream society and was birthed as an "oppressed people" who yearned for a desire to see the glory of God.'[34] Are oppressed people still yearning for the glory of God today? Do we need to rediscover our heritage?

It may not be true for all our churches, but in recent times in some Pentecostal churches there seems to be a toning down of the Pentecostal emphasis. We are seemingly becoming apologetic, nearly apologizing for who we are. The Church must again welcome the Holy Spirit and the manifestations of the Holy Spirit. The recovery of Pentecost is essential to the full range of the Church's life and ministry. Without a powerfully charged and challenging dynamic move of the Holy Spirit, the results can only be inadequate. The importance of the Pentecostal witness for both Church and world cannot be overestimated. Pentecost was meant to be a continuing event.

Others may get it wrong, but let us get our story right, and know our history and our theology.

> Theology provides a critical test for the church so as to determine whether its life and work are consistent with the person and work of Jesus Christ. If the church has no theologians, then it cannot be genuinely self-critical and thereby seek to overcome its short-comings and weaknesses.[35]

We must develop preachers who are thoroughly trained and equipped, who are able to make representation and speak in any forum about their faith without feeling inadequate or inferior.

Very importantly, we cannot afford to neglect the up-and-coming generation. The Church must remain relevantly connected to the times. Mark Sturge admonishes the Church, urging it to address the issues of our youths and not repeat the failures of the past which resulted in the loss of a generation. He pointed out that the Church should never become so occupied that it fails to notice the need for 'new skills, language and interpretive approaches'. 'A church's ability to inspire another generation is almost the litmus test of what will happen to it in the future.'[36]

Conclusion

I conclude with these two quotations:

> The Pentecostals longed for and would not settle for anything less than an experiential manifestation of the Spirit's direct divine, incontrovertible intervention which did not rely on the intellect or feeling but on the sign of the presence of the Holy Ghost which [meant that] both the individual experiencing it and all who were looking on would know that 'the work had been done'.[37]

> Pentecostalism represents a radical Christianity and if it chooses to be at ease and compromise it will fail miserably.[38]

Notes

1 <http://ag.org/top/about/History/index.cfm>.
2 Keith Warrington, *Pentecostal Theology: A Theology of Encounter*, London: T. & T. Clark, 2008, p. 17.
3 'Hermeneutics', in S. Burgess and G. McGee (eds), *Dictionary of Pentecostal and Charismatic Movements*, Grand Rapids, MI: Zondervan, 1988, p. 379.
4 *The Nation*, 28 September 1963, p. 173, cited in Steve Durasoff, *Bright Wind of the Spirit: Pentecostalism Today*, London: Hodder & Stoughton, 1973, p. 7.
5 Durasoff, *Bright Wind*, p. 5.
6 Cited in Gordon D. Fee, *Gospel and Spirit: Issues in New Testament Hermeneutics*, Peabody, MA: Hendrickson, 2006, p. 83.
7 *The Doubleday Dictionary for Home, School, and Office*, Garden City, NY: Doubleday, 1974.
8 James H. Cone, *My Soul Looks Back*, New York: Orbis Books, 1986, p. 69.
9 'Hermeneutics', in Burgess and McGee (eds), *Dictionary*, p. 378.
10 'Hermeneutics', p. 378.
11 'Hermeneutics', p. 378.

12 David J. du Plessis, *The Spirit Bade Me Go*, rev. edn, Plainfield, NJ: Logos International, 1970, p. 40.

13 Robert M. Anderson, *Vision of the Disinherited: The Making of American Pentecostalism*, Peabody, MA: Hendrickson, 1992, p. 90.

14 M. W. Dempster cited in Kenneth J. Archer, *A Pentecostal Hermeneutic for the Twenty-First Century: Spirit, Scripture and Community*, London: T. & T. Clark, 2004, p. 22.

15 Douglas Jacobson (ed.), *A Reader in Pentecostal Theology: Voices from the First Generation*, Indianapolis: Indiana University Press, 2006, p. 5.

16 Jacobson (ed.), *Pentecostal Theology*, p. 5.

17 Anderson, *Vision*, p. 232.

18 'Preaching: A Pentecostal Perspective', in S. Burgess and G. McGee (eds), *Dictionary of Pentecostal and Charismatic Movements*, Grand Rapids, MI: Zondervan, 1988, p. 722.

19 Kenneth J. Archer, *A Pentecostal Hermeneutic for the Twenty-First Century: Spirit, Scripture and Community*, London: T. & T. Clark, 2004, p. 28.

20 Frederick D. Bruner, *A Theology of the Holy Spirit: The Pentecostal Experience and the New Testament Witness*, Eugene, OR: Wipf & Stock, 1972, p. 63, cited in 'Hermeneutics', in Burgess and McGee (eds), *Dictionary*, p. 380.

21 'Hermeneutics', p. 382.

22 Archer, *A Pentecostal Hermeneutic*, p. 69.

23 Gordon D. Fee, *Gospel and Spirit: Issues in New Testament Hermeneutics*, Peabody, MA: Hendrickson, 2006, p. 83.

24 Fee, *Gospel and Spirit*, p. 86.

25 Fee, *Gospel and Spirit*, p. 376.

26 F. L. Arrington, 'Historical Perspectives on Pentecostal and Charismatic Movements', in S. Burgess and G. McGee (eds), *Dictionary of Pentecostal and Charismatic Movements*, Grand Rapids, MI: Zondervan, 1988, p. 378.

27 Gordon Anderson, 'Pentecostal Hermeneutics', *Paraclete: A Journal of Pentecostal Studies* 28 (Spring 1994), p. 13.

28 Fee, *Gospel and Spirit*, p. 86.

29 Fee, *Gospel and Spirit*, p. 86.

30 Anderson, 'Pentecostal Hermeneutics', p. 13.

31 Fee, *Gospel and Spirit*, pp. 85–6.

32 Frank Farrell, 'Outburst of Tongues: The New Penetration', *Christianity Today*, 13 September 1963, p. 5.

33 Arrington, 'Historical Perspectives', p. 387.

34 Cheryl Bridges Johns, cited in Archer, *A Pentecostal Hermeneutic*, p. 18.

35 Cone, *My Soul*, p. 70.

36 Mark Sturge, *Look What The Lord Has Done! An Exploration of Black Faith in Britain*, Bletchley: Scripture Union, 2005, p. 220.

37 Melvin Deiter, 'The Wesleyan Holiness and Pentecostal Movement: Commonalities, Confrontation and Dialogue', paper presented to the Society for Pentecostal Studies on 11 November 1988, cited in Archer, *A Pentecostal Hermeneutic*, p. 18.

38 Durasoff, *Bright Wind*, p. 252.

4

Women in leadership

Introduction

It is a great privilege to be asked to deliver the fourth Oliver Lyseight lecture. As an Anglican theologian I might have hesitated to accept, wondering what I could possibly teach the New Testament Church of God about the Christian faith and witness. But when I heard the subject you had given me, I knew I had to come, for this subject is very close to my heart, and one which I have worked on for many years. I never tire of sharing it with other people.

For this fourth lecture, you have chosen the topic 'Women in leadership'. And women in leadership ought to be a very straightforward and uncomplicated subject to talk about; unfortunately, it is not. For there has been more ferment, inside and outside the Church, about whether women should be leaders, what kind of leaders, and with what scope of leadership, than in almost any other arena. Of course, the topic is neither novel nor radical since women have been in hereditary forms of leadership since history began. To my knowledge, no one has ever questioned why Cleopatra should have been supreme monarch of Egypt, nor challenged the right to authority of the Queen of Sheba. Women ruled then, and have done so before and since. However, most forms of leadership are not hereditary, and in other areas of power and authority a very different pattern has prevailed. Women's leadership has been under contest. Right down the centuries, leadership in the clan, tribe or military, in business, work, professions and religion, has been predominantly male and, even in our own society, it is only over the last hundred years or so that we have seen substantial change. The change has often been brought about as a result of advocacy, which has triggered changes in attitude, social action, campaigns and even civil disobedience. It has been reinforced by legislation. In many other countries these campaigns are still being fought. In Egypt, women protested in front of the State Council Court in Cairo because 25 of them had applied to become judges and had been turned down. They were highly qualified legal experts, but the General Assembly voted to bar women from serving as judges in the court.

Things have changed, however, in the UK where, over the last 40 years, gender divisions between men and women have narrowed substantially as women have moved into areas of work previously occupied only by men. Women now fill some of the highest posts in all the professions. Having overcome the prejudice which held them back from so many jobs, they are now consultant anaesthetists, airline pilots, emergency service supervisors, orthopaedic surgeons. We find their leadership in research, business, public life and science. In fact, today, women head up universities, government select committees and police departments. They are editors of newspapers. They are controllers of radio and television. All this is evident, for the shift has been taking place over decades. The college of which I am a member – Newnham College, Cambridge, one of the last all-women colleges at Oxford and Cambridge – can produce an impressive list of women alumnae who have made an outstanding contribution to the life of the UK and beyond. They are now educating the next generation of women, who expect to reach even higher to make their contribution to society, for there is little doubt that women have as much ability as men to do almost any task required of them.

But you are fully aware of these things and have not asked me here to state the obvious. My task is not to list for you all the gains women have made in leadership in these areas of work and society. For you and I all know that for Christians that is not the issue. The important questions are about who sets the agenda, and what agenda they set, and where we should look to women for leadership. For the Church of Jesus Christ does not and should not take our directions simply from what goes on in a secularized society. In fact, there are many areas where we part company from patterns and policies of contemporary culture, for we believe we have a prophetic ministry. We do not, for example, endorse the right to abortion on demand simply because this is now socially accepted and the right to abortion is protected by law. We do not neglect to discipline our children simply because legislation has given more rights to children and frowns upon too much parental exercise of authority. We do not discourage potential foster parents, just because some local authorities have barred a Christian couple who hold a traditional Christian position on sexual morality. If we were to hold back on sharing our faith in the public arena, because people have been taken to court for offering to pray with people, or wearing a cross at work, we would be abnegating our responsibility. For sometimes our task is also to rebuke society.

So, even though women are now admitted into the highest office in our secular society, it does not mean automatically that the Church should follow suit. The key question for us is not whether the Church must catch up on the progress made for women in the rest of our culture, but what a biblical theology has to say about leadership in the Church and society. Can we be sure, theologically, that the leadership of women is endorsed by faithful Christian exegesis and that the opening up of higher offices in the Church to women is compatible with the word of God? I believe that it is, but I acknowledge that there is a case to be made to convince others. The challenge, then, is not to ape those outside the Church but to find justification for such changes in the New Testament or in the historical praxis of the Church. Of course, when we look at the issue very carefully, we may reach the conclusion that in some areas of social practice, parts of our society have been more biblical than the Church itself!

Inspiration

While we are discussing this, of course, time moves on. History is never static and does not speak with universal clarity. In fact, it offers us a dilemma. Even during those periods when Christian leadership has been predominantly held by men and reserved for men, many women have demonstrated outstanding leadership capabilities. These women have exercised their leadership often against a background of sexism and racism and have sometimes suffered ostracism and rebuff. Yet these pioneering women have been so convicted by the rightness of their cause and so anointed by the Holy Spirit that they have prevailed. Today, we honour them as pioneers in the fight for truth and justice.

We cannot underestimate those African American women of the nineteenth century who showed dynamic and prophetic Christian leadership and social action in the face of great danger. We could focus on Jarena Lee (1783–1850), preaching as long ago as 1810, after a powerful experience of conversion and the empowering of the Holy Spirit; or Maria Stewart, who was speaking and preaching publicly in 1832, convinced that God had called her to be a 'warrior' 'for God and for freedom';[1] or Sojourner Truth, a freed slave whose impassioned oratory of 1851 – 'And ain't I a woman?' – has been remembered for a century and a half;[2] or Harriet Tubman, who brought many other slaves to freedom through the underground railroad in the 1840s and 1850s;[3] or Hallie Quinn Brown, daughter of two former slaves, who became an educationalist and fought for civil rights and universal suffrage from the 1880s to the 1920s. Wherever we look, we see women of amazing courage and authority, whose history must be constantly retold. For their history is ours too, and we need to make it known.

There are also many others who have not made it into our history books. Your very own history in Pentecostalism gives us wonderfully inspirational examples, from the beginnings of the movement in the Azusa Street Mission. For not only were there women active in the evangelism and missionary outreach, but

71

seven of them were reported to be elders of the mission, out of a total of 12. It can have been no accident, of course, for William Seymour himself preached equality and gender inclusion in leadership, and his wife Jenny Seymour, after his death, led the church from 1922 to 1931. This is pioneering stuff. At a time when many denominations were still arguing about whether women had enough talent to be trusted with the flower rota, Pentecostal Christians were sitting under the teaching ministry and spiritual authority of women. Both Lucy Farrow and Julia Hutchins are also commemorated as outstanding prayer leaders and evangelists.

And so it has continued, despite setbacks, retractions, back-lashes, reinforcing theological barriers and indifference, until today, when we have a large witness of outstanding women leaders in every area of the Church, both in the UK and across the world. I want simply to acknowledge the contribution made by some of my own key sisters in the UK Church today in different denomina-tions: women like Dr Kate Coleman, first black female president of the Baptist Union and a fine thinker, writer and preacher;[4] or Rose Hudson-Wilkin, now Chaplain to the House of Commons, but only because the Speaker of the House overruled the white middle-class clergyman who had been the choice of the Dean of Westminster! (When Rose was asked, somewhat patronizingly, by an interviewer, 'Is this the greatest achievement of your career?' she thought for a moment and replied, characteristically, 'My greatest achievement is to be a mother to my children, a wife to my husband, and a priest and friend to the people of God given to my care.' Then she paused and remarked, 'Cleaning up after an elderly parishioner is more important to me than a title.'[5]) What such women often reflect for us is the true servant-leadership which we find supremely epitomized in Jesus.

Objections raised against women in leadership

The argument is often raised, nevertheless, that these are all excep-tional women, and it is only because of necessity that they break the mould and are allowed by God to succeed as leaders. An additional comment is often made that it is useful to have the women around, because we lack the men to do the jobs that God has called them to. So, even though these women may have been granted a measure of divine authority because of the absence or disobedience of the men, this is not extended to all women. That is why, these critics argue, the Church must not lose its nerve but must hold fast to its traditional position, for too much is at stake.

What lies beneath this negative position towards women's leadership? There are often two different kinds of justification which I want to examine. The first justification does not have its origins in theology, but in what is often called 'nature'.

Arguments from 'nature'

The argument goes something like this:

There are clear and obvious natural differences between men and women, differences which are exemplified in the chromosomal structure of male and female. We all know that of the 22 pairs of chromosomes, one pair alone determines the sex of a person. And although there are occasional abnormalities, the vast majority of the human race conforms to this male–female demarcation.

Nature is not only a matter of chromosomes, however. We can also identify differences in anatomy, physiology, hormones, reproductive organs, weight or brain use. We can see the differences played out in gendered examples of physical strength ('horsepower' of men against stamina and endurance of women). They are reflected too in life expectancy (women have greater longevity). Biological differences are very evident in the process of procreation, where men produce the sperm and women the egg, and where women give birth and feed the young. These differences in biology fit the sexes for different roles in society. Men are 'hard-wired' for jobs where independence and risk are necessary, whereas women are 'hard-wired' for roles of nurturing.

From these assertions, it is only a short step to seeing biology as an explanation for many other alleged differences between men and women, including those that involve emotions or reason. Take the issue of competition, for example, which some people argue is essential to business and the workplace. In a contemporary book, *Why Men Don't Iron*, the authors make this striking claim: 'A man enjoys a neurological high when he is faced by competition . . . a woman is not equipped by biology to receive this neurological reward. Indeed, if anything, her reaction to competition will be anxiety.'[6] This glaring stereotype, which draws on so many unexamined assumptions, is taken further, into the task of housework. This is obviously women's work because

> Men have a lower sensitivity to detail, which means he simply does not notice the dust as she does . . . the stale socks and sweaty shirt don't bother him because they are among the pheromone-related smells that women are acutely aware of, but men do not detect.

Or again: 'His lower serotonin level also makes it difficult for him to persevere with a boring chore, because his reward circuitry is not switched on by this sort of tedious activity.'[7] It would appear that women, by implication, *are* switched on by tedious activity and that we love to be bored out of our minds! Even more alarmingly, this same appeal to biological difference is offered as a justification of infidelity:

> Some high t[estosterone] level males do marry, but they are 43% more likely to be divorced and 38% more likely to engage in extramarital sex . . . The conclusion seems obvious. You can have a man, but you cannot have a man who feels, touches, cares and empathises like a woman, not if you want him to stay a man.[8]

Now, not only is this particular statement dangerous and amoral; it is also unscientific, despite the authors' claim that their book is a scientific account of gender. I know of no scientific studies which have taken a sample of men engaged in extramarital sex or adultery and systematically tested their testosterone levels.

The problems with the claims in this book are almost too obvious to state. Gender assumptions are drawn on uncritically and then reinforced – for example, that competitiveness is a good thing and that men thrive on it while women fear it. Or that only those who are boring persevere with tedious chores and so on. The scientific nature of the explanation is grossly overstated, and little evidence is given. But more importantly, the claims reduce our complex human personhood – with its spiritual, emotional, mental, familial, historical, linguistic, ethnic and cultural influences – simply to biology, which is then offered as an explanation for everything. We are presented as biological machines programmed to act and react in certain predictable ways. This inevitably leaves a moral vacuum where even infidelity and promiscuity are justifiable on so-called biological grounds. It fails to realize, however, that though biology is important to who we are, we are very much more than our biology.

Once we have seen the reductionism of this position its limitations are evident. So it is particularly unsettling when the same biological reductionism also comes into Christian discourse. The argument is offered that, since God created nature, he created the different biology of men and women for a purpose. And that purpose is for women to be homemakers, and men to be leaders. (Of course, there is no problem in having male leaders and women homemakers. The problem comes when we argue that *only* men may be leaders and *only* women may be homemakers.)

This argument about the difference in our 'nature' has a very long history in the Church. Ancient Greek philosophers drew a distinction between 'form' and 'matter', where 'form' was the abstract, abiding, rational principle of reality, and 'matter' was the transient, changing, decaying state we pass through. Inevitably, this distinction found its way into the debate about gender. One of the key medieval theologians of the Catholic Church, St Thomas Aquinas, followed Aristotle in the way he saw the difference between men and women. For him, woman became equated with 'matter', which was passive and subordinate, whereas man was more identified with 'form'.[9]

There are other nuances in the same argument. Some see in biology an explanation of differences in men's and women's spirituality.

This is the view of William Oddie, a minister who left the Church of England over the decision to ordain women to the priesthood. He insists, 'It is a clear and consistent assumption that biological differences correspond to differences of spiritual identity.'[10] Clear and consistent? For whom? And even if it is a consistent assumption, that does not mean that it is a well-founded one. Nevertheless, the same theme is repeated by a former bishop of London who again picks up on women's passivity, following Thomas Aquinas. He says, 'The whole world knows that men are associated with giving and women with receiving.'[11]

This might sound like upside-down thinking. For, actually, the whole world is more likely to know that women are very much the givers and that they have given generously to men, to children and to other women throughout history, mostly without counting the cost. So why does the bishop not get it? The answer is that his understanding of gender is dominated by biology and the sex act. In the sex act the man is indeed the giver and the woman is the receiver; biologically, the man 'gives' the sperm to the woman. Again, few of us would find any problem in accepting this obvious truism. But then the bishop leaps to a huge generalization and makes it the description of all relations between men and women. He universalizes a basic biological process into a metaphysical principle which then governs his attitude to women in leadership. In fact, Bishop Leonard takes this further and proposes it as an argument why only men and not women are suited to priesthood. For priesthood expresses fundamental truths about the nature of God which are essentially male – like initiative, action, dominance and eminence. Women are held to be tied to other qualities like passivity, receptivity and nurture by virtue of their role in procreation and are therefore considered unsuited to leadership in the Church. The problem is that this not only leaves us with a warped picture of men and women; it also leaves us with a rather aggressive view of God.

Arguments based on biological difference were used in a different form in Larry Christenson's book on the family which was a best-seller in the 1970s, especially for young couples who were keen to follow a 'biblical' way of raising a family. He insists:

> If a father spends time in traditional, biological female tasks, such as child-care or basic nurture – feeding the children and dressing them – it produces problems for the next generation. Their sons may well grow up not knowing what it means to be a man.[12]

He does not, unfortunately, consider the counter-argument – that, on the other hand, their sons may well grow up to be very secure young men, because they have been brought up by caring, strong fathers who don't feel the task of childcare is beneath them and are not afraid of being involved in mundane roles that involve caring for their children!

Yet another Christian author, Stephen Clark, also encouraged sex-segregated roles in the home, even warning men not to spend too much time in the company of women, and discouraging 'best friend' relationships between husband and wife. His fear was the same as Christenson's – that men will otherwise become feminized and behave 'in a way more appropriate to women'. For Clark, this in turn will lead a man to 'place a much higher emphasis and attention on how he feels and how other people feel'. And this he sees as dangerous, for 'he will be much more gentle and handle situations in a "soft" way.'[13] Once again, generalizations abound and make life difficult for men who are by temperament tender and nurturant. We are also left wondering how this author would evaluate the gentleness of Jesus or understand the compassionate relationships he had with women.

The problems with all these statements echo the problems I outlined earlier. Gender stereotypes are already loaded into the claims about biology, and little evidence is given to substantiate them. The strong counter-evidence is not even considered. Once again, biology is being made to do work it was never meant to do and is offered as a universal explanation which eliminates all the complexities of human life, moral choice and social context.

This leads me to a further observation. There is a huge confusion between what can be explained by biology or sex, and what can more accurately be explained by culture or gender. We can illustrate this by a table (see Table 4.1).

Table 4.1 Distinction between sex and gender

Sex	Gender
Male or female	Man or woman
Biological category	Cultural category
Identify scientifically	Identify socially
Chromosomes, genes,	Roles, expectations, work,
anatomy, physiology,	communication, learning,
hormones, brain use	upbringing, class
Reproductive, genital	Not fixed; flexible
Same in all cultures	Cultural variations

As I have already said, sex can be identified and measured scientifically – in terms of chromosomes. And sex organs contribute to the differences in much of our biological human behaviour, whether that is in urination or procreation! It is women, not men, who give birth and lactate. And this happens irrespective of the culture, language, customs or period that we live in. In that sense, sex offers us relatively little choice; we receive our sexuality as a given, and then the rest follows. Our bodies behave according to the Creation plan which God has built into us, and which is echoed in other parts of Creation.

Gender, however, is quite different. As a cultural category, it offers us much more choice. We *learn* how to behave as men and women, not simply following a *biological* pattern, but adopting ways which are *socially* acceptable. And gender does not have the same predictable manifestation, for cultures are different in what they see as significant for men and women. What is more, gendered behaviour changes over time, and across ethical, regional and class boundaries. What is appropriate for young men in the West Midlands of the UK today can look very different from the expectations which directed the behaviour of their grandfathers, or what is expected of men in

Saudi Arabia. Furthermore, when we look at the jobs women and men hold, or the different ways they are treated in societies, these are rarely accounted for by differences in creation, sex or biology. They are much more likely to be related to the gender assumptions and patterns of power which have become ingrained in public consciousness in a given period or culture. And this is true whether that consciousness is within society or the Church.

Arguments from theology

Although we can deal very adequately with the problems of the biological stereotypes and generalizations, this does not mean that we have settled the issue of women and leadership. To do that, we also need to look at theology. For the more important objections from a Christian point of view are more likely to be those which flow out of a view of Christian theology, the biblical text, history and tradition. You will readily recognize them if I list them here.

1 In the Creation order in Genesis, man was made first and so has authority over woman.
2 The woman is the 'helpmeet' (the Hebrew word *ezer*) which (to some people) suggests inferiority or subordination to the man.
3 Male predominance, and subjugation of women, is assumed in the Old Testament.
4 In the Gospels, Jesus chose only male disciples.
5 In Catholic tradition, the Christian leader is not just a representative of Christ but also needs to be a representation of Christ, namely, to share his physical characteristics.
6 St Paul teaches in 1 Corinthians that women ought to be silent in the churches.
7 St Paul's concept of headship (see Ephesians 5 which describes the husband as the head of the wife) can also be applied to leadership.
8 The authority of teaching men is explicitly forbidden to women in 1 Timothy 2.
9 Throughout the New Testament, there is an assumption of male leadership.

Many people argue that, when all these issues are put together, they present a clear case that men, not women, are created to exercise leadership in the Church, especially higher leadership. I want to turn to these areas now.

Revisiting hermeneutics

The question is: Where do we start to address these issues? I must resist the temptation simply to examine each of them in turn, for before we look at individual texts or passages in the Bible, there is always the issue of hermeneutics to consider. Earlier lecturers in the Oliver Lyseight lecture series have pointed out that we all read the Bible through some hermeneutical lens. There is nothing wrong with this, and to make that observation in no way diminishes the validity of the Bible as the word of God. The Bible remains the word of God however we read or interpret it. But we are finite and limited human beings, and we can get things wrong. Because we always learn within the context in which we live and through the experiences we encounter, these contexts and experiences make up our 'hermeneutical grid' – our process of interpretation which we bring to our reading of the text. Consequently, our hermeneutics needs to be revisited before we look at these questions, so that our answers do not rely on unexamined assumptions which may mislead us.

I can illustrate the power of the hermeneutical lens very simply with one example. A key theologian who greatly influenced the Catholic Church's ideas of sexuality and women was St Jerome. This thinker was a 'desert father' who spent much of his life in contemplation, but also, I suspect, in fear of women's sexuality. We can legitimately draw this conclusion because we have some of the letters he wrote to young women who sought his pastoral advice. The letters often begin in a pastoral way but move quickly into issues which are of a sexual nature. In fact, they reveal an alarming suspicion, which Jerome harbours, of the seductive intentions of these young women – that their actions are often deliberately designed to seduce men. Many contemporary psychologists would find this fear interesting.

My own concern is with something less traumatic and personal, namely with his commentary on the first chapter of Genesis. It contains this odd observation:

> There is something not good in the number two . . . This we must observe, at least if we would faithfully follow the Hebrew, that while scripture on the first, third, fourth and sixth days relates that having finished the works of each, God saw that it was good, on the second day He omitted this altogether, leaving us to understand that two is not a good number because it prefigures the marriage contract. Hence it was that all the animals which Noah took into the ark in pairs were unclean. Odd numbers denote cleanness.[14]

At best, this exegesis is strange. At worst, it is distorted and biased. Jerome leaps from an observation about God's pleasure with Creation to the absurd suggestion that God is not in favour of marriage! He reads even the account of God's Creation of the world through his anxiety about women's sexuality. And he gets this from the fact that because God does not repeat how good everything is on the second day, there must be something wrong with the implications of 'two', which must be its implicit allusion to sexual intercourse! It is extraordinary, all the more because it suggests that sex is so much in Jerome's mind that he even reads it into the days of Creation!

This would be laughable if Jerome had not influenced centuries of tradition of how people approached women and understood marriage. But it does raise the important question about how we should read the Bible. It helps us to recognize that it can be read through many different kinds of eyes. It can be read through revolutionary political eyes which see it as justifying bloodshed and violence. It can be read through 'separatist' eyes which cut faith off from everyday life. It can also be read through eyes which privilege racial or gender concepts, as many feminists have argued for decades. Some writers argue that it is not possible to read the content without recognizing its male bias, for the Bible is in itself a profoundly patriarchal text. In fact, this was the subject of a debate in the early days of feminist theology. The question was raised whether or not the Bible could be 'depatriarchalized' – in other words, read without the offending patriarchal structure. Phyllis Trible, a biblical feminist, wanted to hold on to Scripture, but strip it of its negative patriarchal elements. Mary Daly, a radical feminist theologian, felt this simply would not work. She remarked wryly, 'There would be just about enough salvageable material to make an interesting pamphlet.'[15]

If we do not wish to dismiss the word of God we do need to pay some proper attention to forming better hermeneutics. What map do we use? The analogy of a map is a good one, for a map that works is one that truly reflects what is actually there; it follows the route for us, rather than imposing itself on the route. Similarly, we need, as far as possible, to get our hermeneutical framework from Scripture itself, not from beyond Scripture and then impose it upon Scripture. Hermeneutics gleaned from personal emotion, psychology, culture or politics could well lead us astray.

So mapping out a hermeneutical framework for understanding gender and relationships between men and women is a useful task. But we do not do this from scratch, for the themes which many earlier writers have picked out as disclosing the unfolding story of God's relationship with the world will help us here. The themes of 'Creation, Fall, Redemption, Pentecost, and Final Glory' can throw great light even on the issue of gender and leadership. Let us take some of these themes and see what they have to teach us.

Looking again at Scripture

Women and men in Creation perspective

We start with the first great theme of the Bible: Creation. We find the human creation in Genesis 1.26–27 (NIV1984). There God says, 'Let us make man in our image, in our likeness . . . So God created man in his own image, in the image of God he created him; male and female he created them.'

Then, in Genesis 2, this is filled out for us. The language and scope are different. In chapter 1 we hear God's big commands: *Fiat*, 'Let there be!' – and there was. God is calling a whole world into being out of nothing. Genesis 2 is more poetic, gentle and detailed. We see God scooping the dust of the earth, breathing life into the nostrils, and this dust becomes a living human creature. The implication is clear: we are creaturely. We share so many characteristics with the rest of Creation. Apparently, 95 per cent of our DNA is found in primates and 35 per cent of our DNA is there in bananas! In this account we have both the uniqueness of our created humanness and our similarity with the rest of God's Creation. We are different in that we are also the 'image of God', created in God's likeness, and we have been given responsibility and stewardship over the rest of Creation.

The Creation account also contains the story of the first human naming the animals. In Genesis 2 they are brought before Adam to be identified. We can imagine him going through the list: 'Aardvark, kangaroo, elephant, hippopotamus . . .' All very worthy, but not great companions for Adam. It is here that for the first time in the story God says, 'Something is not good – that the human being should be on his own' (Gen. 2.18, my paraphrase). So the man goes into a deep sleep, and from the structure of one human a second is made and they are differentiated sexually. Why is this account especially important? I think it is because God does not go back to the dust of the earth to make a second human creature, but one becomes two. It surely is an echo of the unity of humankind: woman and man belonging together. We are not fundamentally different, fundamentally other, but we are in unity as fellow and sister human beings. What is more, we need each other. In marriage, man and woman belong together in the same body. As Adam points out, she is his *isha* (woman) to his *ish*. Adam is not naming the woman here, of course, in the way that he names the animals; he is just giving the generic term for 'woman taken out of man'.

And this is where we need to look at the concept of 'helpmeet'. For, contrary to those who read in this idea the notion of woman's subordination, the Hebrew term (*ezer*) implies something very different. It is used to describe not an inferior, but someone who stands alongside the other. In the 21 times it is used in the Old Testament it often carries the concept of power or strength and is generally used of equals.[16] Sometimes it is even used of God, proclaiming him the strength and power of his people.[17] That is the resonance of the term here. The woman, as *ezer*, is not somebody who has been given to Adam as a subordinate to have authority over but somebody who will walk with Adam in the unity of their humanity. It is reinforced by Adam's cry: 'bone of my bones and flesh of my flesh' (Gen. 2.23 NIV). We belong to each other; we are human together!

A few years ago[18] there was a feminist magazine called *Spare Rib* which was a parody of this narrative. The implication was that religious people, especially in the Christian–Jewish tradition, regard women just as 'spare ribs', even as lumps of meat for men's benefit. But that is not what the story is about. It is rather that, having named all the animals, Adam realizes there is none that he can engage with in a close reciprocal relationship. But now, when confronted by the woman, he gives this cry of exultation, joy and bliss.

Understanding gender through a Creation perspective helps us to see how it fits into a larger structure. We are created by God, as significant, purposeful, accountable and creaturely. We are dependent on God, transparent before God, and women and men are loved equally by God. We are described as the 'image' of God; and, like God, we are relational; in our humanness we are in union with each other, needing each other. We are interdependent, made different but similar. We're made for love and compassion, for intimacy and trust. We are unique where we each have individuality, yet we are also communal and need others in our lives. We need people to love us and acknowledge our significance. We are part of Creation while being the guardians of the rest of Creation and charged to seek justice for Creation. Finally, we are made to be integrated in body, mind, spirit and emotion, and made for eternity.

The impact of sin

Sadly, the biblical story of our humanness does not end there, and the scene rapidly changes in Genesis 3.[19] The warning given to Adam not to eat the forbidden fruit is disregarded and, together, Adam and Eve disobey God. We now see deterioration in their relationship. God calls Adam to account for making this bid for autonomy and going his own way rather than God's. Adam has a choice about how to respond to God. He could admit his sin and show remorse, asking for forgiveness. But a different response is given: 'The woman you gave me tempted me and I sinned' (Gen. 3.12, my paraphrase). In one short reply he effectively shrugs off personal responsibility and blames both the woman and God!

In Genesis 3 we read about the consequences of sin: the arduous nature of work, the difficulty of childbirth, and the dominance of men in their relationship with women. It is interesting that sin will impact differently on the man and the woman. God says to the woman, 'Your desire will be for your husband, and he will rule over you' (Gen. 3.16 NIV). Theologians have argued about what that word 'desire' means, whether it refers to desire for mastery or desire for intimacy. But the consequences are clear enough. Male rule and its effects come in to distort the mutuality and reciprocation of the relationship men and women were created to have.[20]

The Creation narrative gave us harmony, mutuality, love, openness and transparency, where man, woman and God walked together. The sin narrative brings in subservience, rule and domination. The consequence of our sin is that evil is opened up and begins to affect every part of our human lives, whether in our culture, communities or churches.

Sin has so many negative qualities. First, it is alienating: it cuts us off from God, other people, ourselves and the rest of Creation. Alienation separates us and closes us down, for we cannot be open if we are sinning. Next, sin is destructive; it cannot build up, but always tears and pulls down; it destroys and brings harm, even ruin. Sin is also distortive. It takes truths, makes them into shady half-truths, quarter-truths, untruths, absolute lies and complete violations. It changes what is honest and open into something that is closed and wrong. Sin is addictive; it controls us; we give ourselves over to it until it takes away our freedom and becomes habitual. Eventually, we can't stop sinning, except through the power of the Holy Spirit who breaks that powerlessness in us. Sin is even structural: it affects societies, and institutions and patterns of governments. It seeps into the way people operate, into the use of money, into structures of banking, economics, work and military power. Sin is also generational: it passes down family lines, so that patterns of stealing, or lying, corruption or domestic violence are transmitted from one generation to another.

Once we understand the strength and the ubiquity of sin, we realize how desperately we need our Saviour, and the power of the Holy Spirit to free us from its relentless grip.

When we read the rest of the Old Testament from this perspective, we can recognize how much of it is a story of sin and disobedience, alongside God's love and mercy. We see it writ large in gender relationships, in passages like the rape of the concubine in Judges 19, or the violation of Tamar in 2 Samuel 13. Whether it is through lies and distortion, manipulation and deceit, lust or sexual violence, we are reminded again and again of the evil we are capable of.

Redemption: promised and delivered

It is with enormous relief, then, that we discover that sin does not have the last word. God's redemption is promised, prophesied about in the Old Testament and delivered by Christ in his death for us on the cross. The full weight of the redemptive work of God is enormous and beyond the scope of this lecture. But we see some of its breadth in the development of gender. A picture of what such redemption might look like becomes evident even in the women in Israel. The actions of Sarah, Rebecca, Naomi, Ruth, Esther or Rahab all point to the power of God working through women. We read of the courage of the Hebrew midwives Shiphrah and Puah, who defied the Pharaoh in not aborting the male children of the women in their care. (Their response to the orders must go down in history as one of the most implausible ever to be uttered in self-defence. They argued that Hebrew women were not like Egyptian women, but delivered their babies too fast for intervention. The Egyptians did not contest it!) There were also the amazing women leaders, whether prophets like Miriam or Huldah (who interpreted the Book of the Law to the insomniac king and prophesied God's judgement on Israel [2 Kings 22]) or Deborah, the judge (described as the 'Mother of all Israel' [Judg. 5.7, my paraphrase]) whose wisdom and right judgements brought peace to Israel for 40 years.

Even though the culture which formed the background of the Hebrew Scriptures was indeed patriarchal, there were so many moments in its history where we can see the promise of redemption in gender relations. In the book of Numbers, and later in 1 Chronicles, for example, we read the story of the daughters of Zelophehad who had been excluded from the allocation of land because their father had no male heirs. They petitioned Moses and Eleazar and the whole assembly for their right to inherit their father's property rights. Moses took their case to God, and was told that their plea was just (Num. 27.1–7). It is an echo of the provisions at the end of the book of Job, where Job confers the same legacy on his daughters as on his sons (Job 42.15). Incidents such as these signify that something different happens in relation to patriarchy which looks towards the redemption of relationships between men and women.

We see this even more clearly in the prophetic vision of gender inclusion which is given by the prophet Joel when he foresees the future:

> And it shall come to pass afterward [says the Lord], that I will pour out my spirit upon all flesh; and your sons and your daughters shall prophesy, your old men shall dream dreams, your young men shall see visions: And also upon the servants and upon the handmaids in those days will I pour out my spirit.　　(Joel 2.28–29 KJV)

This will come by redemption through Jesus, through whom there will be reconciliation in place of alienation, and where the power and love of God will break the chains of addiction, delusion, destruction, distortion and despair. All this becomes possible because of what Jesus has done for us, because he has died for our sins and opened the way back to the Father; and in him we have forgiveness and new life. He has also brought the same redemption into our human relationships. He has broken down barriers between people, so there is neither 'Jew nor Greek, slave nor free, male nor female' (Gal. 3.28 NIV1984), but we can all be one in Christ Jesus with our purpose restored.

The redemption of gender relations is shown with such clarity in the Gospels, where Jesus so frequently cuts across the cultural stereotypes or expectations, and honours women. Whether it is the Samaritan woman at the well, the woman suffering from menstrual abnormalities, or the woman who anoints him, we see them receive freedom and affirmation in their interaction with Jesus. He prevents a woman from being stoned to death by the crowd (her partner in adultery is not sharing the punishment with her) and tells her to sin no more. He uses a generous widow as a role model for his disciples, allows the mothers of Salem to bring their children to him, and defends Mary who chooses to sit and learn from him. It is women who remain at the foot of the cross, women who go to anoint his body, and women who are entrusted with the message of resurrection. In fact, Jesus models something in his whole relationship with women that remains a powerful challenge to us in our churches today.

Pentecost: the coming of the Spirit

The outpouring of the Spirit seals the redemptive work of the cross in the lives of those believers who give themselves up to the grace and love of God. The picture of the early Church in Acts, where believers experience the power and release of the Holy Spirit, is the concrete evidence that Christ's love is effective in our lives. Even the old prophecies of Joel come to pass. And women do indeed receive the Spirit's anointing and move into works of teaching, leading, counselling and prophecy. Philip's four daughters (Acts 21.9) are given a special mention, and the roll call of women who are active sister-workers of Paul occupies a large space in Romans 16. And we too live in post-Pentecost times. The freedom of the Spirit is here today for those women and men who love God and seek his will. The Spirit opens up new horizons in relationships, new understandings of work or economics, new ways of relating to worldly power and rule. Let me quote from my husband's book on how it can affect the way we understand government:

> The gentle rule of God pulls down all kinds of existing powers and structures that glory themselves. God does rule. 'Perhaps', the gospel whispers, 'we do not need wars, weapons, rulers in palaces, leisured elites, and those who run bloated governments for their own purpose. Our rulers can serve. National and ethnic rivalries can cease. Political and economic slavery can end and the security costs of terrorism can fall. People and nations can be forgiven and fresh starts be made before God. Corruption can be replaced by honesty. The meek can inherit the earth and justice can be done.' Ordinary people, when they are allowed to hear, find these messages appealing especially if they've suffered war, faced the oppression of rulers or been downtrodden by self important politicians.[21]

This is so different from the patriarchal, dominant power which characterizes so much of human society. And in this vision, women too come into new freedom. They can share the prophetic insights of Mary in the Magnificat, and rejoice that God is indeed the one who pulls down the mighty from their thrones and exalts those who are deemed to be nothing.

Applying the interpretative framework to difficult areas

So, through this process of developing a hermeneutical framework using key biblical themes, I believe we are able to see the issues I raised earlier in a bigger perspective. We can read Old Testament passages which outline women's subjugation against an interpretative backcloth. Take the assumption of male dominance for example, and how it is illustrated in passages like Judges 19. Here the woman has no freedom of choice, even over her sexuality. She has to endure the indifference of the husband as to her safety, and then the horrors of a gang rape and finally murder. We can, with some authority, insist that this is not a 'Creation story' which endorses male dominance and shows how we should live. It is, rather, a 'sin story' illustrating the sheer depths of our 'fallenness'. It shows the very opposite of how women should be treated. It is a sombre picture of the cycle of sin when people do what is right in their own eyes (see Judg. 21.25), and rather than acceptance, it brings judgement from God.

When we turn to the New Testament, our hermeneutical framework helps us to address other kinds of confusion. It enables us to grasp more of what St Paul is teaching about women. For Paul was living and preaching after Pentecost and giving us a picture of redemptive relationships, and how women and men can be fully released to experience the Spirit of God.

How do we decide what is Paul's teaching on women in leadership? There are two versions which we are often offered. The first is that women should be silent in the churches (1 Cor. 14.33–35), that women should not teach or have authority over men (1 Tim. 2.12). The second is that in Christ there is no male or female but barriers are broken down, and women are on equal ground to men (Gal. 3.28), that the Church should accept the leadership of women, based especially on the example of Phoebe (Rom. 16). Further evidence is offered that women should pray or prophesy (1 Cor. 11.4–5), though in that culture they should do so with their heads covered to avoid misunderstanding. These two positions are different, but they both appeal to the same Bible.

So what sense do we make of this conflict? Does St Paul take us towards endorsing women in leadership or prohibiting it? A careful hermeneutical framework helps us to see that Paul is speaking into both the sin and redemption chapters of our story.

In effect, he is working out both the constraints of our sinful condition and the implications of Pentecost in the way we should live in the Church. For example, in 1 Corinthians 14 he is talking about order in worship. He is arguing that what we need in the Church is the sort of orderly worship which both enables us to experience the eruptive power of the Holy Spirit and allows us to hear what God is saying to the Church. So, as well as being releasing, worship must also be disciplined. It is in this context that he asks women not to 'speak'.

The word he uses is very important. It is not the words used for prophesying, preaching or praying. It is *lalein* – the word most usually associated either with chattering, or speaking in tongues. This offers two interpretations of what Paul is saying. One is that women are asked not to speak in tongues, which seems very unlikely, as Paul offers no other restrictions on the gifts of the Spirit other than a need for order which is required of the whole congregation. The second is that women are asked not to chatter. This seems far more likely, as the instruction is followed by the remark that if there is anything they want to ask their husbands, they should ask them at home. Yet being required not to spoil the worship by unnecessary chit-chat or distracting people from concentrating on God's word is very different indeed from being prohibited from speaking prophetically or pastorally in a gathering of Christians.

Similarly, hermeneutics helps us to understand that we have to hold together what Paul says and what Paul does. In Galatians 3.28 Paul states a truth which he has fought for in his ministry, that the old divisions between Jew and Gentile are broken down in Christ. So Gentile converts do not need to be brought under the law, or circumcised, in order to be accepted as Christ's followers. Yet this great truth does not stop Paul from having Timothy circumcised! Even though Paul opposes those who insist on the circumcision of Gentiles, for he believes it implicitly denies the centrality of the cross, the half-Greek Timothy undergoes circumcision. Why? The answer seems to be that Paul simply recognizes that others will resist the radical nature of Christian freedom, unless there is some concession to patterns which are familiar to them. Some will not accept Timothy's ministry unless he is seen to be 'as Jewish as the rest of us'. So, in order to safeguard Timothy's ministry while the Church struggles for maturity, Paul quietly puts aside the principle he embraces in Galatians 3.28.

This has very similar implications for women's ministry. For it is not only a division between Jew and Gentile that Paul sees as eradicated in Christ. He also addresses the division between male and female. For that is superseded now that we are one in Christ. So he releases women into the liberty of ministry in the gospel: he releases Priscilla into a teaching ministry (she and her husband, Aquila, are part of Paul's own teaching and tent-making team), commends Phoebe to the Roman church and greets many women sister-workers in the gospel (Rom. 16.1–16).[22] But at times, he also restrains women. He says they are to learn in submission.

Placing Paul's teaching in the context of Paul's practice also helps us to understand these passages. In particular, we could take the difficult passage of 1 Timothy 2, the only place where women are asked not to teach. For many critics of women's leadership, this is decisive, for they are expressly prohibited from having teaching authority over men. The Greek word is *didasko*, which people read as referring to public or official teaching. People interpret this to mean that if women do teach, it must be in a women-only context, not an authorized public ministry. Yet we have the example in the Acts of the Apostles of a woman teaching a man. For Priscilla is described as teaching Apollos (Acts 18.26) along with her husband, Aquila. Apollos himself will be a leader in the New Testament Church, but his knowledge is deficient. People try to get round this by claiming that Priscilla is not really 'teaching'. But exactly the same word is used as in 1 Timothy 2: *didasko*. It is clear, also, that she exercises this ministry with Paul's approval, for he describes her and her husband as his 'co-workers' (Rom. 16.3 NLT). So, at the very least, we are left with the fact that a woman can teach, and that whatever is intended in 1 Timothy 2, it cannot be a universal ban.[23]

As a postscript, it is interesting that Paul chooses those three particular divisions as his examples in Galatians 3.28. It would be very familiar to a Jewish readership. I was visiting a Jewish synagogue, and my host was interpreting the Hebrew readings and prayers for me. I suddenly heard a prayer which I recognized. The man praying was thanking God that he was not a Gentile, a slave or a woman! 'This is no disrespect to you, as a Gentile and a woman,' my host pointed out with some haste. 'It is just that it is such a great privilege to be born a Jewish man, for it carries deep responsibilities.' It is so striking that Paul addressed this centuries ago. He was effectively telling his readers that Jewish free men have no higher status before God than Gentile slave women, because in Christ barriers are eradicated and we are on level ground. The amazingly radical nature of this truth has still to penetrate the Church.

Conclusion

It is time to move away from biblical exegesis and ask, 'What kind of women should be encouraged to move into Christian leadership?' The answer has to be, 'Those who are called by God and who know Christ's saving grace in their lives.' Beyond that, they must occupy the leadership roles which resonate with the gifts that God has given them. For there are many forms of ministry, and God will continue to equip women to fill those roles where they are needed. We need women who can exhibit the fruit of the Spirit in their lives; those who have love, joy, peace, patience, kindness, goodness, faithfulness, humility and self-control. We need women with the gifts of the Spirit: gifts of pastoring, teaching, discernment, wisdom, tongues, prophecy, healing, rebuking, generosity and hospitality. We need those who can model servant-leadership and live with gratitude; those who are powerful enough to take the lead and show the way, but can also cope with discouragement. We need women who don't allow resentment to take root in their lives but can return with forgiveness and with joy and with blessing;

those who can go out to others with healing, rather than with anger; can bring the love of God and the power of the Spirit into broken lives and painful relationships. Above all, we need those who love both God and people and can show those who are estranged from God something of the compassion and grace that is there in Christ's outpouring of himself on the cross.

The leadership of women can be a powerful challenge to our Church and our world. But it may require much rethinking among those who are the Church's current leaders. For they need to have the will and the vision to pray for it, resource it and release it, so that the whole body of Christ can be effective in its witness to God.

Notes

1 Jane Johnson Lewis, 'Maria Stewart: Abolitionist, Public Speaker, Writer' <http://womenshistory.about.com>.

2 See the biography by Patricia McKissack, *Sojourner Truth: Ain't I a Woman?*, New York: Scholastic, 1994.

3 Kate Clifford Larson, *Bound for the Promised Land: Harriet Tubman, Portrait of an American Hero*, New York: Ballantine, 2003.

4 Kate Coleman, *7 Deadly Sins of Women in Leadership*, Birmingham: Next Leadership, 2010.

5 Jennifer Lumley, 'Interview with Jamaican Rev. Rose Hudson-Wilkin, Chaplain to the House of Commons', 13 September 2010 <www.jamaicans.com>.

6 Bill and Anne Moir, *Why Men Don't Iron: The Science of Gender Studies*, London: HarperCollins, 1998, p. 192.

7 Moir and Moir, *Why Men Don't Iron*, p. 255.

8 Moir and Moir, *Why Men Don't Iron*, p. 265.

9 St Thomas Aquinas, *Summa Theologica* (trans. Fathers of the English Dominican Province), London: Burns, Oates and Washbourne, 1914.

10 William Oddie, *What Will Happen to God?*, London: SPCK, 1984, p. 33. See also my review in the *Scottish Journal of Theology* 41 (1988), pp. 117–24.

11 See Graham Leonard, 'The Ordination of Women: Theological and Biblical Issues', *Epworth Review* 11/1 (January 1984).

12 Larry Christenson, *The Christian Family*, Minneapolis: Bethany Fellowship, 1970, pp. 17–18.

13 Stephen B. Clark, *Man and Woman in Christ*, Ann Arbor, MI: Servant Books, 1980, pp. 636–49.

14 St Jerome, *Tract against Jovinian*, quoted in Jane Barr, 'The Influence of St Jerome on Medieval Attitudes to Women', in Janet Martin Soskice (ed.), *After Eve: Women, Theology and the Christian Tradition*, London: Marshall Pickering, 1990, p. 96.

15 Mary Daly; see the critical anthology by Sarah L. Hoagland and Marilyn Frye, *Feminist Interpretations of Mary Daly*, University Park, PA: Pennsylvania State University, 2000.

16 Deut. 33.29; see also Joseph Coleson, *Ezer Cenegdo: A Power Like Him: Facing Him as Equal*, Grantham, PA: Wesleyan/Holiness, 1996.

17 For example, Exod. 18.4; Pss. 120.1–2; 124.8.

18 From 1972 to 1993.

19 See the commentary on Gen. 3 in Catherine Clark Kroeger and Mary Evans, *The Women's Study Bible*, New York: Oxford University Press, 2009.

20 For an analysis of some of the passages which describe violence towards women, read Catherine Clark Kroeger and Nancy Nason-Clark, *No Place for Abuse*, Downers Grove, IL: IVP, 2005.

21 Alan Storkey, *Jesus and Politics*, Grand Rapids, MI: Baker, 2007, p. 119.

22 Of the 27 Christian leaders greeted by Paul in this passage, ten are women. They include 'Junia' who is described as part of an apostolic couple.

23 For a fuller discussion of this passage and of Priscilla, see Margaret Mowczko, 'Did Priscilla Teach Apollos?', in *Mutuality and Unity in Christ* <http://equalitycentral.com/blog/?p=171>.

5

Youth culture: friend or foe?

CARVER ANDERSON

Introduction

I count it an honour to greet you all today, as friends, workers, ministers, pastors, theologians, men and women of God, seeking to make a difference in your respective contexts.

It is indeed a privilege to be invited by Revd Phyllis Thompson and her board to deliver the fifth Oliver Lyseight Annual Lecture. As I understand it, these lectures are intended to explore issues and themes that confront black Pentecostal leadership in the twenty-first century. Of course, these issues can also be pertinent within a white or ecumenical leadership framework. So for us today, this lecture seeks to explore issues of youth culture and its expressions that may impact churches and communities across the UK.

Before exploring these issues, let me briefly reflect on the previous lectures. They commenced with Dr Joe Aldred setting the scene by examining the theme, 'The challenges of black Pentecostal leadership in the UK in the twenty-first century'. Dr Aldred argued for a 'stand-out' church leadership that has the ability and capacity to lead people into a fruitful future. The second lecture was by Dr Robert Beckford, who considered the theme, 'From maintenance to mission: resisting the bewitchment of colonial Christianity'. He emphasized the need for the Church to develop a meaningful political theory for working within marginalized communities. Revd Ruthlyn Bradshaw explored the issues associated with Pentecostal hermeneutics in the third lecture. She argued for a Church that would have the courage to explore hermeneutics as a tool for interpreting scriptural text in relation to meaning, both historically and within a postmodern context. In the fourth lecture, Dr Elaine Storkey considered 'Women in leadership'. It was clear from her paper that Dr Storkey very much supported and embraced the notion that women are fully commissioned by God with gifts to maximize the potential of churches and communities.

All of us, in addressing the overall theme, 'Challenges of black Pentecostal leadership in the UK in the twenty-first century', add to the rich Oliver Lyseight tapestry that weaves together a commitment to mission with sacrificial service. In *Forward March* he says,

> In June 1956, I received a letter from the Missions Board stating that they had appointed me as State Overseer of the work in England; that I should give up my manual labour and go full-time to preach out new churches within the country.[1]

For this fifth lecture, I have been asked to address the topic of youth culture and specifically the challenges associated with this and how our churches may seek to respond. These responses are grounded in the combination of community service and self-sacrifice made manifest by Oliver Lyseight and all the other pioneers of black Pentecostalism in the UK. I wish to acknowledge from the outset the rich history and legacy from which the New Testament Church of God has emerged. This is highlighted in the New Testament Church of God fiftieth year celebration magazine:

> The New Testament Church of God has a rich heritage. Courageous men and women of God have laid the foundation and planned the strategies for its growth in the 1950's and 1960's. They did so despite racism, marginalization and rejection. They refused to be so silent and dared to sing the Lord's song in a strange land. As a result of their faithful service and the devotion of loyal followers, we now have a denomination that is firmly set in the Pentecostal tradition.[2]

I am indeed humbled to state that without the pioneering work of some of our mothers and fathers, this legacy on which we continue to build may not have been possible. May their respective contributions and uniqueness serve as models, as reflective lessons encouraging the Church to move towards greater relevance and contextual impact in communities and areas ravaged by the 'evils' of disaffection, poverty, homelessness, marginalization, teenage pregnancy, youth violence and antisocial behaviour, gangs, guns and knives, educational crisis and unemployment.

This lecture seeks to build on that legacy. It seeks to develop a framework that will enable us seriously to consider how we engage young people (churched and un-churched) during these times of evil. I intend to map this by reflecting on the past and assessing the present context, developing a greater understanding of both, and proposing strategic interventions. This will enable our theological reflection and exploration, and suggest a strategic framework for revised practice and action associated with young people. My approach here draws on insights gained from a consideration of what has been called practical theology. This model for doing theology is represented in the 'pastoral cycle' proposed by Paul Ballard and John Pritchard (see Fig. 5.1).[3]

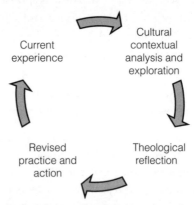

Figure 5.1 The pastoral cycle (Ballard and Pritchard)

Setting the scene: do young people matter?

As we share this time together, I wish to acknowledge the many families and friends who have lost young people. These young people were taken from us through senseless violence and attacks. We remember Rhys Jones (Liverpool), Anthony Walker (Liverpool),

Ben Kinsella (London), Stephen Lawrence (London), and Charlene Ellis and Latisha Shakespeare (Birmingham), just to name a few. Some of you here may still be grieving the loss of a youngster also 'gone too soon' – I am. It is not easy to bear, I can assure you. I can also assure you that, whether these young people belong to our communities or not, their loss is our loss and the pain of their families should also be our pain. Many of us saw Doreen and Neville Lawrence express their grief at the sentencing of the two men accused of Stephen's murder, albeit 18 years on. Many of us grieved with them.

There are times when I reflect on my own history and the issues that I encountered as a youth and have to thank God for life. There were times when my family thought they had lost me to the culture of the 'streets' or the 'world'. Our fellowships and churches are not immune to the threats and impacts of the 'streets'. How then do we as Christian leaders and concerned individuals seek to make sense of a 'street culture' that is ever more confusing, conflicting, violent, engaging and secular?

I would be very naive to suggest that there is a simple answer to this. However, a first step needs to be an understanding of the world of young people as we experience and describe it and as the young people themselves see it and experience it. For example, Patrick Regan, in his exploration of young people and gang culture, suggests that

> What our young need are individuals who are willing to get involved, to step out of their own world in order to relate to those in a different position. If we are not faced with violence of gangs on our doorsteps everyday it is easy to forget about them, but we need to open our eyes to the state of our society. It is easy to make assumptions and judgments about other people's lives. We can look at violent teenagers and criticize them for their choices, or we can try to see the world from their perspectives. That does not mean we are in any way condoning their actions, but we will never be able to help them if we watch from a distance and simply judge.[4]

In our attempts to understand and respond to youth culture 'on road', we are faced with a number of inherent difficulties, contradictions and dichotomies regarding the perception, definition and experience of young people. We are faced with understanding the multidimensional influences on our young people, and our role as one voice among many, potentially competing in a youth-culture marketplace for the attention of young people.

Having said that, it is my experience that the majority of young people cope quite well with the challenges of life and are generally well balanced. It is important to acknowledge and affirm this. The recent cross-government report on ending gang and youth violence states:

> The vast majority of young people are law-abiding citizens who make a valuable contribution to society and their local community. In fact young people are disproportionately more likely to be the victims of violence and to worry about the impact of it on their day-to-day lives. British Crime Survey estimates suggest that young men aged 16 to 24, for example, are more than four times more likely to become the victim of violent crime than the general population.[5]

Over the years, we have had groups and organizations that developed a specific focus on young people. These include the Prince's Trust, Youth for Christ, the YMCA, Scripture Union, Pathfinders, Urban Saints and the Christian Youth Club movement, just to name a few.[6] While acknowledging the need for these groups and the work that they have done, we are arguably faced with a world motivated by secular forces and motivations that influence our young people and their choices and go beyond these established ways of looking at and working with them.

One marketing expert, Peter Zollo, suggests that:

> There is no age group more involved with trend setting than teens. Not only are teens trend setters for one another, they are also trend setters for the population at large. Teen influence extends beyond fashion and popular culture, affecting the nation's economy in a big way.[7]

According to market researchers, the most influential of all the trendsetters is the disaffected minority teenager, particularly the urban black male. These researchers argue that, drawing upon their 'street' and prison experiences, our young people have created raw and irreverent music-based cultures that marketers describe as a cultural triangle of fashion, music and sports. Marketing studies found that

> this urban youth culture has a major impact on consumer prefer-
> ences in the general market in the United States and worldwide in
> a wide range of industries, including apparel, footwear, soft drinks,
> packaged foods, personal care products and all facets of the enter-
> tainment industry.[8]

Given the real and tangible challenges facing young people, their families and communities today, I suggest that we are at a critical point right now. If our churches' influence and impact in communities becomes further diminished, we are faced with the increasing possibility of greater disaffection and marginaliz-ation, especially for those who are associated with the Luke 4.18 text (MSG):

> God's Spirit is on me;
>   he's chosen me to preach the Message of good news to
>   the poor,
> Sent me to announce pardon to prisoners and
>   recovery of sight to the blind,
> To set the burdened and battered free.

I am mindful that many of you may be attached to groups and churches with active youth programmes which seek to develop relevant and meaningful spiritual and physical activities that engage primarily with young people who are church-affiliated or are at least responsive to what the Church offers. These young people may not have been seen in the uprisings or riots that ravaged our towns and cities in August 2011. However, it does not mean that the influences and temptations to be involved were not present for them. I am aware of families and friends of church leaders and members who are attending court because a young family member has been involved in criminally orientated activities and lifestyles.

I suggest to us, today, that the recent riots across the UK should be seen as a wake-up call for our churches. We need to wake up in terms of our theological responses to the issues that daily impact the individuals, families and communities whom we seek to serve.

The British home secretary, Theresa May, said:

> One thing that the riots in August did do was to bring home to the entire country just how serious a problem gang and youth violence has now become. In London one in five of those arrested in connection with the riots were known gang members. We also know that gang members carry out half of all shootings in the capital and 22% of all serious violence. And even these shocking statistics may underestimate the true total. Similar figures for the riots were recorded by West Yorkshire Police, while Nottinghamshire had only a slightly lower figure. Most other police forces identified fewer than 10% of all those arrested as gang members. But the fact that so many young people, who are not involved in gangs, were still willing to carry out such serious acts of violence and disorder in the summer merely reinforces the urgent need to deal with youth violence. For too long, government action has not been as effective as it should be at stemming the violence. We need a long-term, evidence-based programme to get a proper grip on gang and youth violence.[9]

The critical question at this juncture is: Has the Church or the Christian community got a responsibility to engage with young people associated with our churches and those that are un-churched or marginalized? In considering this question and the answers, I wish briefly to explore some biblical texts and to suggest some clear mandates.

The Church – called to be 'salt' and 'light'

As many young people question the validity of spirituality and church, we are faced with competing forces within a very secular context when we proclaim Jesus as 'Wonderful Counsellor, Mighty God, Everlasting Father, Prince of Peace' (Isa. 9.6 NIV). There is enough evidence to suggest that the Church as an institution does not exist for or by 'itself'. It exists for the glory of God and to bring salvation to the world. It exists to reveal the good news that Christ left in it to the world. I suggest that Jesus was quite clear about this and laid out the Church's *raison d'être* when he told his disciples, 'You are the salt of the earth . . . You are the light of the world' (Matt. 5.13–14). It is with this mandate that our churches in their various settings are commissioned to minister and bring salvation to our world, with all its many contradictions, philosophical positions and ideological aspirations.

The concept of 'spirituality' requires understanding in this context. We need to understand, within a theological framework, how secularism and postmodern thinking regarding morals and ethics have influenced the way human life is expressed by individuals, families and communities. Research by the Heythrop Institute for Religion, Ethics and Public Life suggests that 'spiritual' does not necessarily mean 'religious'. The Institute suggests that the use of 'spirituality' by the secular world does not necessarily enable Christians to construct a useful bridge to the searching secularist. When we use the same words, we probably don't mean the same things.[10]

Having acknowledged this, I suggest it is important to frame and affirm our focus on Christian spirituality and, more specific-ally, Pentecostal spirituality in our exploration of transforma-tive ministry. I argue, furthermore, for a practical-theological or applied-theological framing. I introduced a model for practical theology earlier. James Woodward and Stephen Pattison suggest that pastoral–practical theology is a place where religious belief, tradition and practice meet with contemporary experiences, ques-tions and actions, and conduct a dialogue that is mutually enriching, intellectually critical and practically transforming.[11]

The need to develop such a Pentecostal urban praxis, one that is relevant, cutting edge and practical, has been an issue since the urban uprisings and riots that occurred in the UK in the 1980s. It is my suggestion that if we are to be advocates of the Christian faith in community, then we are faced with the need to consider more specifically the work of the Holy Spirit as a 'change agent' relevant to the needs of marginalized people and communities.

Revd Joel Edwards, a previous general director of the Evangelical Alliance, argues for a Church and theology that represent new ways of engaging with contemporary urban situations. He advocates a 'radical rethink on how the church represents the gospel (good news) within the communities they are part of'. He argues:

> And if we are to be good news, people should identify us not with our campaigns or concerns but with Jesus himself. If evangelicals fail in this they fail in their mission. That mission is not to win political points in the public square; it is to present Christ as a credible Saviour to society, and we should be unmistakably identified with him.[12]

Clearly, Edwards is highlighting the need for evangelicals to seek to be relevant within the communities of which they are a part. This is both in terms of a focus on non-radical (and I would argue, non-traditional Pentecostal) readings of Scripture that support particular ways of life, and a movement from countless declarations of intent to meaningful Spirit-driven interventions.

Our challenge, therefore, is to establish an understanding regarding the Holy Spirit's capacity to influence the release, transformation and reformation of communities and young people held captive by 'principalities and powers', in Classical Pentecostal theological terms, and deemed 'hard to reach', 'disaffected' and 'hard core' in the language of community intervention.

The concept of the Holy Spirit as 'change agent' or 'change advocate' is seen in numerous biblical texts. This way of understanding the work of the Spirit drives my current work in urban mission. Theological reflection is directly and organically linked to community-based intervention. How we understand the work of the Spirit shapes how we work in communities and the goals of that work.

For example, much recent urban mission reflection and intervention in the UK has been driven by 'white' theologies of incarnation, justice and compassion derived from non-Pentecostal traditions. As the work of Oliver Lyseight and many others show, black Pentecostals in the UK were essentially urban missionaries. It is part of our legacy, our inheritance, to proclaim the good news in places where others fear to tread, among those whom others fear. We did not need to draw on the reflections and theologies of others to recognize the work of the Holy Spirit as a 'change agent' for promoting service for the common good.

However, I have concerns regarding our drift towards gospels of affluence and prosperity affirmations. These seem to understand the work of the Holy Spirit in ways that are different from and are in some ways contradictory to those of our Pentecostal pioneers, such as Oliver Lyseight. These gospels of prosperity and affluence have in some cases led to aspirations towards self-indulgence as opposed to self-sacrifice, to enrichment rather than service. It is within the above context that I wish to reclaim the radical urban roots of Pentecostalism as represented by the Azusa Street Revival of 1906.

Power for service in the community

- *Mark 1.8* 'He will baptize you with the Holy Spirit';
- *Matthew 28.19* (NIV) 'Go and make disciples of all nations';
- *Luke 24.49* (NIV) 'stay in the city until you have been clothed with power from on high';
- *Acts 1.4–5* 'the Promise of the Father'; 'you shall be baptized with the Holy Spirit';
- *Acts 2.4* (NIV) 'All of them were filled with the Holy Spirit and began to speak in other tongues';
- *Acts 10.44–47* 'the Holy Spirit fell upon all those who heard the word'; 'the gift of the Holy Spirit had been poured out'; 'these [people] . . . have received the Holy Spirit';

- *Acts 19.1–6* 'Did you receive the Holy Spirit?'; 'the Holy Spirit came upon them, and they spoke with tongues and prophesied';
- *Acts 2.43* (NLT) 'A deep sense of awe came over them all, and the apostles performed many miraculous signs and wonders'.

These and associated texts indicate that the Church's mandate for urban witness can be arguably linked to the power given by the Holy Spirit. The task of engaging with young people of this generation is by no means easy, but it is the task Jesus called us to through his words and example. When he called us to make disciples of all people, he did not just mean those people who make us feel safe and comfortable.

Cultural contextual analysis and exploration

In my attempt to offer some thoughts and insights regarding work with young people and associated cultural issues, I wish to thank those young people and leaders who have contributed to my research and exploration. This includes working with some of the most disaffected young people and families in cities within Great Britain, such as Birmingham, Nottingham, Brixton and other parts of London, Leeds, Sheffield, Wolverhampton and Liverpool. These theological reflections have been complemented and developed through dialogue with those involved in urban mission and community intervention in the USA, Jamaica, Northern Ireland and South Africa. I have to acknowledge my debt to these sisters and brothers. There have been many difficult times in my own work and research. Research based on participant observation can be exhausting emotionally, physically and spiritually. These young people and leaders contributed to my continued development and helped to equip me regarding an evolving youth-cultural paradigm.

It is my view that the competing challenges that face young people in the twenty-first century are like those facing no other generation in history. Young people in our churches and communities are the products of Western rationalism and secularism. They are bombarded and engage daily with many of the following:

- social media and telecommunication (Facebook, YouTube, Skype)
- the fashion and beauty industry (magazines, film, TV)
- sexual liberation and sexuality issues
- secular spirituality (African, Eastern, postmodernist)
- gang, post-code and territorial challenges (social exclusion)
- family and relationship challenges (domestic violence, abuse)
- violence and antisocial behaviour
- drug and substance use and misuse
- struggles with faith, the Church and Christianity
- music and role models from the industry
- mental health and emotional challenges
- inequalities and oppression (race, gender, religion)
- racial and cultural identities
- financial challenges.

As a result of the above, many young people may struggle to maintain consistency and stability. This can result in them finding themselves in one or more of the following positions, which I develop in related writings and perspectives:

- in, looking in (church-focused);
- in, looking out (churched young people with outside influences);
- out, looking in (un-churched with church influences);
- out, looking out (un-churched and classed as 'hard to reach');
- in and out, looking in (churched young people involved in 'contradictory' lifestyles);
- out and in, looking out (un-churched with church family affiliations).

A leading Birmingham criminologist's research on 'hard to access' young people supports the argument for the development of a strategic and holistic model for working with young people. He suggests that

The absence of holistic approaches in addressing the core factors of young people's distress is a major contributory factor towards the isolation they feel from the community at large. Many young people have wandered aimlessly through school and community, sometimes blind, sometimes hitting the mark, but never really knowing how well they've done, or are still doing. Many young people have been cheated at not having their own parents around to assist and guide them into adulthood. This has resulted in strong feelings of low self-esteem, self-doubt, and emotional paralysis. This, in turn, has had a domino effect by throwing them into turmoil, and projected rage.[13]

There is much evidence from government select committees and church and community sector research that shows that young people are plagued by such challenges in twenty-first-century Britain. It also shows that young people's responses to these challenges and their lifestyle expressions can have profound effects on wider society.

The seriousness of the situation is acknowledged in a London Safeguarding Children Board document, in which the board highlights concerns relating to reports of 169 youth gangs in London. According to police intelligence, a significant proportion of gang members had used firearms in crimes and were estimated to have been responsible for around 40 murders and 20 per cent of the youth crime in the UK capital. In 2007, 27 deaths were attributable to youth gang-related shootings or knifings.[14] The board also suggests that the emergence of a violent youth subculture can be further fuelled by the following factors:

- high levels of deprivation (neighbourhoods which would benefit from regeneration and a higher police profile);
- neighbourhood destabilization (families moving due to refurbishment or a rapid change in the population profile), which weakens the ties of kinship and friendship and the established mechanisms of informal control and social support;
- grooming and recruiting by peers, relatives and friends on behalf of older men and other gang leaders;

- poorly performing schools in terms of leadership, positive ethos and proactivity, and ability to work in partnership;
- high levels of exclusions and truancy among children with a negative attitude towards school and also particular educational difficulties;
- lack of affordable youth facilities;
- emergence of a culture/value system which idolizes or legitimizes violence as a means to resolve conflicts and gain 'ends' (specific community areas).

This analysis, I suggest, identifies key features of life in most of the UK inner cities. It also, I would suggest, offers a basis for churches to consider their own analysis and exploration in the areas that they serve. It is clear, though, that this framework looks at the challenges from the outside. It is clear that we also need to understand how they are experienced and understood from the inside.

Over the last 30 years there have been two to three generations in some communities that have grown up seeing each other (children, parents and grandparents) experience disaffection, brokenness and hopelessness. These experiences have their roots in the consistent failure of public authorities in education, health, police, prisons, social care and employment. Too many people feel distracted, disappointed and depressed by the unwillingness of those in positions of influence and authority to listen to them. All this can be bound up with, I would suggest, the lack of community responsibility, social exclusion, poor housing, racism and many other factors. These things work together to limit the lives of those to whom the Spirit of God calls us to preach and minister: the imprisoned, the poor, the blinded, the broken and the battered (Luke 4.18–19). These things have led to at least two, and in some cases three, generations of families experiencing isolation, lack of trust and 'imprisonment' in lives of crime.

Cavalli-Sforza and Feldman explain this type of action as 'cultural transmission', an intergenerational transaction between two groups of people living within the same cultural environment.[15]

According to cultural transmission theory, in the socially dis-organized and poorest zones of a city, certain forms of crime and antisocial behaviour become the cultural norm. This accept-ance is then transmitted from one generation to the next as part of the normal socialization pattern. Successful criminals and their lifestyles provide role models for the young, demonstrating both the normality of criminal behaviour and the possibility that crime may pay.

The key observation at this juncture is that, despite 30 years of policy making, community responses and faith representations and millions of pounds of regeneration initiatives, the challenges, problems, injuries and aspirations remain the same. Rather than focusing on the past and considering the persistence of these things at this point, let us look forward and ask each other two funda-mental questions:

1 Is it possible for the Christian community to bring transcendent hope and action through the application of a practical theology?
2 Is the Christian community able to work with young people and communities characterized by a culture that offers little or no hope?

Dr Robert Beckford argues that some churches have attempted to 'fix' some of our youths, hoping that they will be 'better'.[16] His argu-ment is that young people who become disaffected are the products of a systemic failure or multiple breakdowns in social, cultural, political, communal and moral forces in the urban context. His argument echoes the London Safeguarding analysis of inner cities and the experiences of some of the people who live there.

While acknowledging that Beckford's approach and analysis are grounded in a necessary socio-political evaluation, I would argue that it is necessary but insufficient in terms of offering a framework for black Pentecostal engagement with urban mission among young people in twenty-first-century Britain. I would argue that as black Pentecostals we should look for a greater emphasis on the 'principalities' and 'powers' referred to in Ephesians 6.12.

I would suggest we should seek to make sense of whatever principalities and powers are influencing this generation of young people. These forces also, it has to be said, shape our daily battles to be the Christian witnesses that Jesus mandated us to be, especially when we are to be witnesses to young people who are un-churched, marginalized and labelled 'hard to reach'.

Given the complexity and challenges outlined so far, it has become more urgent for us to consider ways to engage, understand and support young people in their quest to live productive lives. We need to do this in the knowledge that we do not fight against 'flesh and blood', but principalities and powers. We need, I would argue, to consider a practical Pentecostal theology that takes into account the power of the Holy Spirit to transform lives and relationships in particular contexts. Based on my own experiences and reflections, this theology needs to be grounded in young people being supported to 'work out their own salvation' within spaces and places that represent a theology of liberation.

Perpetua Kirby summarizes the benefits of involving young people in being a part of their own contextual solution as follows:

- youngsters can offer quality data to enhance understanding of their needs;
- young people speak a common language;
- young people raise issues with other young people that they would not have done with an adult;
- young people can be encouraged to own what they express, do and plan;
- young people presenting their own issues can have greater impact with audiences.[17]

It is within the very complex issues already highlighted that I wish to explore another crucial challenge facing our communities, and indeed the Church. This relates to the over-representation of black young people in the criminal justice system, in school exclusions, in deaths both as a result of gang-, gun- and knife-related incidents, and as a result of police custody.

Black young men – myths and realities

According to Barrow Cadbury, the over-representation of 'Caribbean young men and increasingly Muslim young men in the criminal justice system signifies the need for an overhaul of a system which so clearly puts criminal justice before social justice in the pathway to adulthood'.[18] This conclusion is supported by the Just Justice study, carried out by The Children's Society, into black young people's experience of the youth justice system. The study was specifically constructed to

> listen to and take account of young black people's life stories and experiences of being young, black and involved with the youth justice system, and by doing so to gain deeper understanding of the issues surrounding this particular group of young people.[19]

It is interesting and at the same time very depressing to see similarities with the USA. The Black Youth Project Chicago aims to raise the voice and profile of young people. It states:

> When one looks at a wide array of some of the most controversial and important issues facing the country, African American young people are often at the center of these debates and policies. Whether the issue is mass incarceration, affirmative action, the increased use of high-stakes school testing, HIV and AIDS, sex education in schools, or welfare reform, most of these initiatives and controversies disproportionately impact young, often vulnerable, African Americans. However, in contrast to the centrality of African American youth to the politics and policies of the country, their perspectives and voices generally have been absent from not only public policy debates, but also academic research. This research project will fill that void, placing African American young people at the centre of our analysis and action.[20]

It is important to note two things. The first is that those who feel the brunt of social, political and economic changes are those who have least say over them. Black young people are effectively silenced by the ways in which the 'system' works. Given its persistence, it is arguable whether this silencing is a side effect or an accident. The second is the fact that, while black young men and increasingly young women are over-represented in the youth justice system, this does not necessarily or simply indicate a higher level of offending in general. The relationship is complex, and includes potential areas of discrimination. This complexity was acknowledged by the 2007 House of Commons Home Affairs Committee report on young black people and the criminal justice system.[21]

Within the past ten years the UK has experienced the emergence of a growing body of evidence that suggests that gang-related violence, including the use of guns and knives, and antisocial behaviour have reached epidemic proportions in certain areas of our cities. While acknowledging the very real fear that the issue of gun- and gang-related crime can generate in communities, regardless of race, spirituality, class or status, I intend here to make reference to London and Birmingham, where the black communities are adversely affected. Similar points could be made about communities in Nottingham, Manchester, Bristol and Leeds, or any other inner city in the UK.

There has to be a note of caution, however, in that it could be argued that to concentrate on one particular ethnic group can possibly be seen as stigmatizing. While this is a valid notion, there is no denying the fact that in some of our cities about 60–70 per cent of gun-related murders and shootings involve what is categorized as 'black-on-black' violence.[22] This has led to the emergence of 'targeted' responses: police operations directed at black communities. For example, there is Scotland Yard's Operation Trident in London and the Birmingham Reducing Gang Violence Partnership in the West Midlands. Operation Trident was established to deal specifically with gun crime in the black community, whether by Africans, Caribbeans or British-born blacks. This is an important issue that the Church cannot turn away from with any kind of integrity. It is the reality of the road, a reality that we have to find the tools to respond to with grace, courage and imagination.

Dr Cheron Byfield, a leading UK educationalist and director of The National Black Boys Can Association, places the emphasis more on what enables black young men to succeed rather than on the forces that oppose and disable them. Her study, *Black Boys Can Make It*, follows 40 young black men in universities in the USA and the UK. These young men, argues Byfield, could have entered a spiral of crime. She highlights the fact that, even though most of the young men had experienced backgrounds characterized by absentee fathers, inadequate housing, low teachers' expectations, peer pressure to reject education as 'uncool', racism and stereotyped negativity, their lives show that black boys can and do succeed.

This capacity for success, Byfield suggests, can be put down to a combination of the following factors and characteristics:

> Personal ambition, parental support, empathic teaching, willingness to learn, self-belief and self-confidence, acknowledgement of the value and benefits of educational achievements, a determination to work their way out of poverty, developing a competitive nature and life-style, not allowing distractions or disparagement even from friends and peer groups to deter them from achieving their personal goals and, above all, taking personal responsibility for organising their lives and not looking to blame others for any of their shortcomings, failures, disappointments and setbacks.[23]

According to Martin Glynn, approaches to young people are successful when they combine knowledge, empathy, positive reinforcement and a non-judgmental attitude. In *Hard to Access Young People and Drugs Support Services in Birmingham* he argues that

> Young Black people have felt comforted by talking to someone who identifies with who they are, as opposed to their supposed social label. Likewise, disaffected White males and females who are embracing urban culture through music such as hip-hop, garage, drum 'n' bass, dancehall music, etc. have felt more at ease knowing that the researcher had a familiarity with the world they occupy. At all times positive reinforcement without judgment enabled those young people to feel at ease in expressing their views on their terms.[24]

If we are seeking as churches to be more deliberate and radical in our witness in communities plagued by a culture where young people are increasingly seen through lenses of 'them and us', we need to take seriously Byfield's and Glynn's observations. These observations need to be built into our theological and pastoral reflections. I firmly believe that such practical-theological considerations should be at the heart of how churches deal with the intensifying challenges facing the youths and communities we seek to serve.

Theological reflection towards developing revised action

Over the past ten to fifteen years we have seen many Pentecostal and independent black- and white-majority churches emerge in some of the UK's most deprived communities. However, the question is: What impact do these churches have in the lives of the young people, families and children around them? From my research sample, I am aware that some of our churches remain detached and inconspicuous in areas where much help and hope is required. This is a cause of deep concern. There seems to be little of the pioneering spirit of Oliver Lyseight in some of our congregations. I wish that it were not so.

In all humility, I would ask that we consider our history as black Pentecostals and the needs of the people we have been mandated to serve. This, I suggest, requires the leadership to commence a series of theological, organizational and self-reflections as to the meaning of our Pentecostal presence and relevance in inner cities and outer estates. Jesus commissions us to be 'salt' and 'light'. What does this mean for us in twenty-first-century Britain? How then can we develop a model where transcendent hope and action are manifested through a practical-theological paradigm?

Writing in a time of great darkness, murder and persecution, Dietrich Bonhoeffer, a German practical theologian, wrestled with the meaning of the Church. He reflected on the mandate of the Church and wrote of its mission to a broken world.

The church of Jesus cannot arbitrarily break off all contact with those who refuse His call. It is called to follow the Lord by promise and commandment. That must suffice. All judgement of others and separation from them must be left to him who chose the church according to his good purpose, and not for any merit or achievement of its own. The separation of church and world is not effected by the church itself, but by the word of its calling.[25]

In the same spirit, African American theologians James Cone and Gayraud Wilmore make the point that the responsibility of black churches is to be both spiritually and socially relevant to the communities they serve or are a part of. However, they argue that 'Mainline black churches, however exclusive they may seem to outsiders, are usually located in the heart of the ghetto'.[26] Their mission, then, is to be relevant to, and part of, the people in the heart of the ghetto. Many churches have been faithful to this mission.

For Cone and Wilmore, this means that we need to acknowledge the part played by these churches in relation to the many issues faced by some urban communities. The Church has a history of working with communities to challenge racial inequalities, social and political marginalization and disempowerment, and violence and crime. To illustrate this relationship, Cone and Wilmore tell the story of how un-churched urban youths identified with 'their church' during the 1965 Watts Rebellion in Los Angeles.

During the rebellion, a gang from another side of the city entered the vicinity of a prestigious black Presbyterian church and threatened to burn it down. At this point the young people from 'on road' who lived in the community, most of whom had never entered the church, protected the building. They stated to the rival gang, 'If you wanna burn down some white folks' church, that's hip, but this is our church, and you ain't messing with it. Understand?'[27] Cone and Wilmore report that the church was left unmolested.

Cone suggests that black pastors and church members may complain about burglaries, broken glass and vandalism; however, there is an understanding that their churches belong to the neighbourhood in which they stand and cannot but identify with the 'weal and woe' of the impoverished masses with whom many of them have little intercourse. This is of profound importance to our reflections. Our presence is a statement, a declaration of belonging. Whether we like it or not, our churches and fellowships may well be identified with areas we no longer live in or people with whom we would not choose to associate. Cone says that the black Church is inseparable from the ghetto and that whatever motivates the ghetto to peace-making or rebellion must motivate the black Church to action.

The Watts scenario is not dissimilar to the Handsworth, Birmingham riots of 2005. During the time of the riot, a church was filled to capacity for a community meeting relating to an allegation that a young African Caribbean woman had been raped by a group of Asian males. At the time of the meeting there was word that Asian youths were planning to attack it. Within a few minutes of this information becoming public knowledge, a number of un-churched youth, some affiliated to local gangs, sought to defend the meeting and the people in it. This led to two nights of rioting in Birmingham, resulting in the deaths of two young people.

An important question to consider at this juncture is: How can churches and communities dialogue and work together to create a paradigm for *shalom* and hope, given the challenges faced by third- and fourth-generation black communities? Babatunde Adedibu helps us here, suggesting that black-majority churches are evidently more proactive now regarding working together. He states:

> This growing level of engagement in strategic high-level politics is emerging in numerous ways, significantly through the work of the Black Christian Leaders' Forum (BCLF) which is a consortium representing African and Caribbean Christians in the United Kingdom. The BCLF have met with the Prime Minister and departmental secretaries on a wide range of issues with respect to the black community.[28]

However, the response and reality for many un-churched urban youths is that churches are not relevant to their context. This is not because they have no need of the good news about Jesus, no need of Spirit-filled transformation, no need of *shalom* or hope. It is because church people judge and disregard them and the meanings that they give to their lives. It is because we have forgotten our black Pentecostal roots and our mission to serve the poor, the disabled, the broken, the battered and the imprisoned.

I would indeed say that we, as leaders, have a wealth of resources that can strengthen our quest to be relevant and cutting edge in the communities we serve. If we are to engage our youths, then we should aim to develop a specific practical-theological approach for working with them. We can work to create a model that gives an opportunity for our people to critically reflect on their own practices, their responsibilities in their fellowships and the effectiveness of their organizations.

Eric Brown, the administrative bishop of the New Testament Church of God, has sought to critically reflect upon and review the organization's relevance. He has developed a strategy that could position the Church for more relevant impact. This strategy was implemented as a sevenfold vision in 2006, with the acronym 'Big Move':

- Building confident and committed leaders;
- Informing and impacting our youth;
- Growing healthy churches;
- Mobilizing our Church for ministry and missions;
- Offering hope and leadership to our communities;
- Valuing our women and our men;
- Evangelizing our communities and our world.[29]

This is a workable strategy. We need to make it work. The futures of our mission and our communities rest on being able to make it work. To do that, we have to review and reflect on it in terms of critical outcomes and evidence-based instruments. We need to take it that seriously. We need to work together on what we want to achieve, by when and how we might achieve it, and know whether we've been successful or not.

There are at least two models that we could use to do this important work. The practical-theological spiral we discussed earlier offers one. Many of us are familiar with this way of planning in one form or another. It fits in with many of our assumptions and values. Another model, one with which we might be less familiar, is that of cultural competence. The National Centre for Cultural Competence (NCCC) embraces a conceptual framework and model for achieving cultural competence adapted from the work of T. Cross et al.[30] Cultural competence requires that organizations and their personnel have the capacity to:

- value diversity;
- conduct self-assessment;
- manage the dynamics of difference;
- acquire and institutionalize cultural knowledge;
- adapt to the diversity and cultural contexts of the individuals and communities served.

I want to suggest here that, while these capacities may feel secular and slightly uncomfortable, they do offer an approach to the issues that values the contributions and experiences of those the Church seeks to work with and minister to. This, as I've suggested throughout this lecture, is profoundly important. A persistent weakness of policy making or interventions regarding black and urban communities is their failure to recognize the young people's aspirations. They have consistently refused to affirm that black boys and girls can and do succeed. They have refused to see the goal-striving patterns of black youth and to measure these in relation to the social and political ambitions and the real opportunities available to community individuals as a whole.

If our interventions do not address the historical and contemporary conditions that create and maintain poverty, inequality, gang affiliation and youth violence, we open ourselves to the challenge that we are inadvertently supporting the continued marginalization and deprivation of communities already disadvantaged and broken. It is therefore important for us as black Pentecostals to recognize the possibility and opportunities to be 'salt' and 'light' in the places and spaces we occupy, whether it be within our families, communities or churches. Jesus' story of the Samaritan and the man left for dead at the roadside makes this clear. Those who walked by on the other side were not 'sinners', but the 'righteous' (Luke 10.30–37). Importantly, Mark Sturge suggests that black-majority churches have emerged to be change agents in some communities. He states that

> The overwhelming evidence is that they are hubs of many communities, and they are the most cohesive representation of the Black community. They continue to provide essential services for community development, ranging from counselling and advice services to care and advocacy for older people.[31]

Reframing: a conclusion as a new start

It is clear, then, that wherever we are positioned today, it is important to be open and prepared for transition. So where are you? Where am I? Where are we? For me, let me say that openness to change has been a challenge. Reframing my action and practice, my thinking and feeling, is never easy, as Pauline, my wife, will gladly testify. Yes, I like to think that I am right!

However, the challenge facing us now is such that I wish to embrace Dr Robert Beckford's call for change. He suggests that the Christian Church is required to be more prophetic in its ministry towards the community, especially disaffected youths. He argues that the prophetic approach is the only viable way of creating a counter-cultural, politically engaged and self-sacrificing worshipping community. Such a community, he says, will be able to transform both itself and the disaffected and marginalized in urban Britain.[32]

This, I firmly believe, was Oliver Lyseight's vision when he was asked to give up his manual work and preach full time. He wanted to see a new thing built here in the UK by the power of the Holy Spirit. Along with the other pioneers, he stepped out in faith and threw himself into setting the foundations for black Pentecostalism as we know it now. I would suggest that they were practical theologians in the sense that they lived what they believed and did God's work wherever they were for the common good and the glory of God.

I would want us to embrace that tradition, embrace it and extend it. This lecture is generally rooted in a practical-theological paradigm. I am motivated to encourage us to seriously consider developing greater insights into ways of thinking about and doing God's work wherever we are. It allows us to bring current practices, experiences, values, beliefs and concerns of church communities, and indeed wider society, into critical dialogue with Christian theological and scriptural traditions and processes, leading to practical action.[33]

Today has been part of that process. We have examined some key themes around the Church's responses to an evolving youth culture. We are faced with complex interconnected issues which require us to consider carefully how we should approach them.

The first step is to talk honestly and openly. In our discussions and conversations, we need:

- to remain open to new thoughts and ideas, as these may be catalysts for developing more engaged and community-orientated churches, where help can be asked for or offered regardless of a person's membership status;
- to remember the empowering nature of Pentecostalism in the pursuit of relevance and effectiveness;
- to work towards an evidence-based theology and mission that reaches out in partnership and a spirit of engagement to the wider community;
- to establish and reaffirm youth engagement forums within the churches, so that young people and their contemporary expressions of faith can influence church policies, procedures and projects.

Notes

1 Oliver A. Lyseight, *Forward March: An Autobiography*, Wolverhampton: George Garwood, 1995, p. 51.
2 Leony Titus and Sharon Gordon (eds), *New Testament Church of God: Celebrating Our Past, Charting Our Future – 50 Years in His Service*, Northampton: New Testament Church of God, 2003, p. 55.
3 Paul Ballard and John Pritchard, *Practical Theology in Action: Christian Thinking in the Service of Church and Society*, 2nd edn, London: SPCK, 1996, pp. 85–6.
4 Patrick Regan and Liza Hoeksma, *Fighting Chance: Tackling Britain's Gang Culture*, London: Hodder & Stoughton, 2010, p. xv.
5 Home Office, *Ending Gang and Youth Violence: A Cross-Government Report Including Further Evidence and Good Practice Case Studies* (Cm. 8211), London: The Stationery Office, 2011, p. 16.
6 David Hilborn and Matt Bird (eds), *God and the Generations: Youth, Age and Church Today*, Carlisle: Paternoster Press, 2002.
7 Peter Zollo, *Wise Up to Teens: Insights into Marketing and Advertising to Teenagers*, 2nd edn, New York: New Strategist, 1999, p. 8.
8 Robert Brown, Ruth Washton, *The U.S. Urban Youth Market: Targeting the Trendsetters*, New York: Packaged Facts, 2000 <www.packagedfacts.com>.
9 Home Office, *Ending Gang and Youth Violence*, p. 3.
10 James Hanvey, *The Spirituality of Leadership*, London: Heythrop Institute for Religion, Ethics and Public Life, 2008.
11 James Woodward and Stephen Pattison (eds), *The Blackwell Reader in Pastoral and Practical Theology*, Oxford: Blackwell, 2000, p. 9.
12 Joel Edwards, *An Agenda for Change: A Global Call for Spiritual and Social Transformation*, Grand Rapids, MI: Zondervan, 2008, p. 95.
13 Martin Glynn, *Hard to Access Young People and Drugs Support Services in Birmingham*, Birmingham: Birmingham City Council Drug Action Team, 2004, p. 9.
14 London Safeguarding Children Board, *Safeguarding Children Affected by Gang Activity and/or Serious Youth Violence*, London, 2009 <www.londonscb.gov.uk>.
15 L. L. Cavalli-Sforza and M. W. Feldman, *Cultural Transmission and Evolution*, Guildford: Princeton University Press, 1981.

16 Robert Beckford, *God and the Gangs*, London: Darton, Longman and Todd, 2004.

17 Perpetua Kirby, *Guide to Actively Involving Young People in Research: For Researchers, Research Commissioners and Managers*, Hampshire: INVOLVE Support Unit, 2004.

18 Greg Parston et al., *Lost in Transition: Young Adults and the Criminal Justice System*, London: Barrow Cadbury Trust, 2005, p. 3.

19 David Wilson and Gwyther Rees, *Just Justice: A Study into Black Young People's Experiences of the Youth Justice System*, London: The Children's Society, 2006, p. 56.

20 Black Youth Project, *Exploring the Attitudes, Actions, and Decision Making of African American Youth by Highlighting Their Lives, Ideas and Voices*, Chicago: University of Chicago Centre for the Study of Race, Politics and Culture <www.blackyouthproject.com/wp-content/uploads/BYP-Research-Summary.pdf>.

21 House of Commons Home Affairs Committee Report (HC 181-I [Incorporating HC 1675-i and ii, Session 2005–06]), *Young Black People and the Criminal Justice System*, London: The Stationery Office, 2007.

22 Graeme McLagan, *Guns and Gangs: The Inside Story of the War on Our Streets*, London: Allison & Busby, 2005.

23 Cheron Byfield, *Black Boys Can Make It: How They Overcome the Obstacles to University in the UK and USA*, Stoke-on-Trent: Trentham Books, 2008, p. x.

24 Glynn, *Hard to Access*, p. 19.

25 John W. de Gruchy, *The Cost of Discipleship: Dietrich Bonhoeffer*, London: SCM Press, 2001, p. 132.

26 James H. Cone and Gayraud S. Wilmore, *Black Theology: A Documentary History, vol. 1: 1966–1979*, New York: Orbis Books, 1979, p. 15.

27 Cone and Wilmore, *Black Theology*, p. 15.

28 Babatunde Adedibu, *Coat of Many Colours: The Origin, Growth, Distinctiveness and Contributions of Black Majority Churches to British Christianity*, Gloucester: The Choir Press, 2012, p. 184.

29 Titus and Gordon (eds), *New Testament Church of God*, pp. 55–6, cited in Barrington O. Burrell, *African-Caribbean Church Culture: The Evolution of Black Majority Churches in Britain*, London: Grosvenor House, 2011, p. 33.

30 T. Cross, B. Bazron, K. Dennis and M. Isaacs, *Towards a Culturally Competent System of Care*, vol. 1, Washington, DC: Georgetown University Child Development Center, CASSP Technical Assistance Center, 1989.

31 Mark Sturge, *Look What The Lord Has Done! An Exploration of Black Christian Faith in Britain*, Bletchley: Scripture Union, 2005, p. 109.

32 Beckford, *God and the Gangs*, p. 7.

33 Howard W. Stone and James O. Duke, *How to Think Theologically*, 2nd edn, Minneapolis: Fortress Press, 2006.

Further reading

Anderson, C. 'Where There Is No Youth the Vision Will Perish.' *Black Theology: An International Journal*, no. 6 (2001).

Beckford, Robert. *Dread and Pentecostal: A Political Theology for the Black Church in Britain*. London: SPCK, 2000.

Cone, James. *Speaking the Truth: Ecumenism, Liberation, and Black Theology*. Grand Rapids, MI: Eerdmans, 1986.

Edwards, Joel (ed.). *Let's Praise Him Again: An African-Caribbean Perspective on Worship*. Eastbourne: Kingsway, 1992.

Grant, Paul, and Raj Patel (eds). *A Time to Speak*. Nottingham: Russell Press, 1990.

Grant, Paul, and Raj Patel (eds). *A Time to Act*. Nottingham: Russell Press, 1992.

McDowell, Josh, and Bob Hostetler. *Right from Wrong: What You Need to Know to Help Youth Make Right Choices*. London: Word, 1994.

Conclusion

PHYLLIS THOMPSON

If this compendium challenges you to reflect critically on your own sense of calling and practice of ministry then we will have gone some way towards achieving our aims.

As indicated, in general, leadership training programmes in the black-majority churches have been variable. We are still riddled with many misguided, misplaced, self-selected 'leaders'. We are also challenged to look at the demography of our local communities and ask some hard questions:

- What in the name of God are we doing here?
- How far does the local church reflect the community?
- How well does the leadership engage with the powerful and the powerless?
- How effective are we in our global and digital world?
- Are we going to stay in our 'holy huddles' and use our effort to maintain the past or do we take the courageous step forward in our effort to lead the people of God?

These lectures accentuate the fact that people need to feel secure with their leadership and encourage a leadership that demonstrates more than charisma: a leadership, rather, that demonstrates Christian integrity, pastoral sensibility and theological credibility.

They each underline the view that our churches require a leadership that is informing, engaging, empowering and inspiring; in other words a leadership that is fully equipped to model the Christian message as a trustworthy alternative to the worldviews of our postmodern world.

They highlight the need for every leader to become more intentional in the pursuit of excellence in church leadership. As ever and in contradiction to customary views, the Church has a vital role to play in communities.

In her book, *Bothered and Bewildered: Enacting Hope in Troubled Times*, Ann Morisy puts it this way:

> The idea that Christians can help the world to change for the better sounds increasingly ludicrous. Whilst Christians might have confidence in the transformational capacity of the Christian faith, few others do. In fact, more and more seem inclined to think just the opposite: that those who see their faith as a force for good in the world are not just plain deluded, they are dangerously deluded.[1]

Pastors and key leaders have the responsibility to ensure that they are living the message in their practice of ministry. Our rallying call should probably be the need to actively pray for divine insight to be righteously subversive.

Learning from our history for the benefit of all is an important concern as we better equip ourselves to address the challenges of our time. The truth embodied in the statement attributed to Johann Wolfgang von Goethe, 'We don't know what we see; we see what we know', would best serve as a caution in all our endeavours.

The lecturers are clear that the demands of postmodernism require a rigorous appraisal of the precepts on which we build our models of leadership:

- Joe Aldred calls for a more mature and responsible leadership engendered by insights from critical scholarship;
- Robert Beckford makes a plea for active engagement in the development of a theology that is pedagogical and politically constructive;
- Ruthlyn Bradshaw argues for credible, confident and inspiring church leaders who are informed by the theological discipline of Pentecostal hermeneutics;
- Elaine Storkey proposes the mapping of a hermeneutical framework for understanding gender and the relationship between men and women as a useful task;
- Carver Anderson makes a case for leadership strategies that enable transformative ministry.

Each lecture illuminates concerns and indicatives for formative ministerial training, continual ministerial development and whole-church learning.

In the aim to build on our legacy and raise the standard of leadership, the New Testament Church of God is exercising an approach to learning that provides opportunities for personal development and the ministerial development of our emerging and practising leaders. The learning events include taught sessions, conferences and seminars, and an increasing tendency towards coaching and mentoring, internship and supervised learning, as well as learner-led groups such as learning networks and study circles.

We recognize the critical stage at which our denomination has arrived in our pilgrimage here in the UK. The lectures provide significant insight into some of the tensions, constraints and opportunities that we as a denomination encounter as we seek to position ourselves in the mission and ministry of the wider Church in the UK.

We are clear about the value of partnership in ministry. The image of the kingdom community, as given in Romans 12 and 1 Corinthians 12, is foundational to the concept of our vision to grow disciples at all levels and status within the institutional Church in order to fulfil the goals of Luke 4.18–19:

> to preach the gospel to the poor,
> . . . to heal the brokenhearted,
> To preach deliverance to the captives
> And recovery of sight to the blind,
> To set at liberty those who are oppressed,
> To preach the acceptable year of the LORD.

It is our ambition to contribute to church leadership learning and development that will positively challenge our current ways of thinking and doing church. In building on our Pentecostal tradition and the legacy of our pioneers, our aim is to facilitate opportunities for leadership development that are rigorous enough to raise the standard of church leadership and enable us to play our role in the transformation of society until Christ returns.

At a recent senior leaders' development training event, I asked for their expectations and gathered the following:

- to learn something I don't know;
- to gain some practical ministerial insight;
- to learn from the vast experience of my peers;
- to gain knowledge that will help me grow to the next level of leadership;
- to be affirmed in the things I am already doing;
- to increase understanding of a pastoral approach that best matches the changing world of the twenty-first century;
- to enhance skills to communicate with the current generation;
- to think outside the box;
- to critically assess my role and identify opportunities for growth;
- to have the opportunity to reflect on current practice of ministry and formulate effective strategies to move forward;
- to gain necessary tools to be a better leader;
- to learn more effective ways to manage leadership teams;
- to share fellowship;
- to sharpen focus.

I was particularly heartened to note the expectation 'to think outside the box' – this involves imagination, courage, creativeness and vision. According to John Maxwell, leadership is at its best, in fact it becomes a reality, when it has evidence that it actually adds value to someone's life. A leader who is intent and open to his or her own 'becoming' will be a leader who is free to allow the 'becoming' of all. Christian leadership training must be specifically intentional and targeted to assist church leaders to become 'fit for purpose', to use contemporary parlance. Critical reflection and robust and challenging conversations are important starting points in the process, as is the commitment and willingness of the leaders themselves to assume the responsibility in putting theology and leadership development as a priority in their growth plan for effective Christian ministry.

Our purpose is to facilitate a rigorous, structured process of leadership training and development for those engaged in the critical role of church leadership in the UK today. We are committed to leadership training that is sustainable; training that enables the leadership to become firmly grounded in Christian wisdom and compassion; training that will take us forward in the interest of the personal, spiritual and organizational dimensions of leadership enrichment and the enhancement of practices of Christian ministry. We want to develop committed and courageous leaders. We want to clarify the leadership models and framework for Christian leadership training and development that would best enable us to minister effectively to the current generation. To this end, we gladly welcome opportunities for partnerships and links with those who share our theological stance and mission aspirations.

Note

1 Ann Morisy, *Bothered and Bewildered: Enacting Hope in Troubled Times*, London: Continuum, 2009, p. 11.